Betty Crocker's

Bread Machine

cookbook

Macmillan • USA

MACMILLAN
A Simon & Schuster Macmillan Company
1633 Broadway
New York, NY 10019-6784

Library of Congress Cataloging-in-Publication Data
Crocker, Betty.
    [Bread machine cookbook]
    Betty Crocker's bread machine cookbook.
            p.   cm.
    Includes index.
    ISBN 0-02-860367-2 : $9.95
    1. Bread.   2. Automatic bread machines.   I. Title.   II. Title:
Bread machine cookbook.
TX769.C737   1995
641.8'15—dc20   95-4973
                                                                 CIP

For consistent baking results, the Betty Crocker Food and Publications Center recommends Gold Medal flour

Manufactured in the United States of America
20   19 18 17 16 15 14 13 12 11
First Edition

Cover design by Iris Jeromnimon
Book design by Michele Laseau

Preceding Page: Pumpkin–Whole Wheat Bread (p. 41)
Contents Page: Harvest Loaf (p. 18), Sticky Orange-Almond Rolls (p. 17)
Front cover: Honey Sunflower Loaf (p. 35)
Back Cover: Wild Rice Breadsticks (p. 72), Double Apricot–Almond Bread (p. 49), Fireside Cheddar-Olive Bread (p. 27)

Contents

Introduction *4*

Perfect Bread Machine Baking *5*

1 Classic and Savory Loaves *13*

2 Special Grains and Sweet Loaves *37*

3 Breads in All Shapes—Savory and Sweet *59*

4 Terrific Toppings *81*

Index *93*

Introduction

Bread machines have really modernized the way we bake bread—in just a few easy steps, you can have fresh bread whenever you want! Whether for the dinner table or a gift for friends, homemade bread is always welcome wherever you go, conjuring up warm and friendly feelings. We have made it easy to prepare bread perfect for ever occasion, whether it is sliced up for sandwiches or made into breadsticks. We've collected some of the most appealing—and easy—bread ideas that are sure to inspire you when you'd like to entertain as well as give you ideas for everyday breads.

Looking for some great sandwich bread? Try Classic White, Multigrain Loaf or Pumpkin–Whole Wheat for a change. Looking for bread with some extra zip? Bake up some Pesto-Tomato Bread, Garlic-Basil Bread or Double Mustard–Beer Bread. Hungry for something sweet or a little bit different? You'll enjoy Coffee-Amaretto Bread, Spicy Apple Bread or Blueberry-Lemon Loaf. And who can resist freshly baked breakfast goods? Serve Cinnamon-Raisin Bread, Sticky Orange Rolls or Fruited Coffee Cake and everyone will be ready to rise and shine.

Need a quick pizza crust or calzone or want to whip up a focaccia? That's no problem as we've also included doughs to mix, shape and bake. There's also an entire chapter on delicious spreads and jams to complement your breads. You'll find ideas for sandwiches, how to use up your leftover bread, information on how to cut and store your bread and a whole trouble-shooting guide so your bread will always be perfect. We know you'll agree that this is the book you'll turn to for every occasion!

Betty Crocker

Perfect Bread Machine Baking

5 Steps to Perfect Bread

1. **Read All Instructions Carefully**

   Read your bread machine manual carefully, especially the tips and hints. They can provide a good troubleshooting guide should your bread not come out perfectly. Understand how your machine cycles work, and use them properly. Do not reset the machine in the middle of a cycle. Although you can check the dough while it's mixing, never open your machine during the rising or baking stages to check the progress because the rising loaf could collapse.

2. **Assemble Your Machine Correctly**

   Make sure the pan, blade and other parts are correctly assembled for proper mixing and kneading. If the bread machine parts are used incorrectly, the dough may not mix, knead, rise and bake properly.

3. **Read Your Recipe**

   Understand the recipe you are making before you begin to use your machine. Be sure to use only the ingredients called for, and measure them carefully because over- or undermeasuring can affect the results.

   - Use standard household measuring cups and spoons for all ingredients.

   - To measure bread flour, spoon into standard dry-ingredient measuring cup and level with a knife or spatula.

   - To measure liquid, pour into see-through liquid measuring cup, place cup on flat surface and read measurement at eye level.

4. **Prepare Ingredients before Baking**

   Assemble ingredients, measuring carefully, before putting any of them in the machine. For best results, ingredients should be at room temperature except for those ingredients normally stored in the refrigerator, such as fresh milk and eggs. Check the recipe carefully to be sure that all of the ingredients have been added in the proper order.

You can choose the delay cycles (if your machine has them) for recipes that do not contain meats, eggs or fresh dairy products or fruits and vegetables (so that bacteria won't grow while these ingredients stand in the machine for several hours). When using a delay cycle, be sure the yeast does not come in contact with liquid or wet ingredients.

5. **Adjust Recipes One Change at a Time**

   As you become familiar with your bread machine and find a favorite recipe, you may get the urge to experiment by changing the ingredients. If you do experiment with reliable bread machine recipes, make just one change at a time so you know what does or does not work. Also see the Guide to Great Bread (p. 8) for ingredient amount recommendations.

Glossary of Bread Ingredients

Flour is the primary ingredient, by amount, in yeast bread making. When mixed with liquid and kneaded, the proteins in the flour form *gluten*, which stretches like elastic and traps bubbles of gas formed by the yeast to give bread its cellular structure.

Bread flour: A special blend of wheats higher in gluten-forming protein than all-purpose flour. Bread flour absorbs greater quantities of water and produces a more elastic dough, resulting in tall, well-formed loaves. It is the best choice for bread machine baking.

All-purpose flour: A blend of selected wheats suitable for all kinds of baking. Unbleached and bleached varieties are available. All-purpose flour can be used in bread machines, but because it contains less protein than bread flour, bread volume will be somewhat lower and the texture slightly coarser than breads made with bread flour.

Whole wheat flour: Made with the complete wheat kernel. Stone-ground whole wheat flour is coarser than roller-milled whole wheat flour. Breads made with whole wheat flour have a nutty flavor and dense texture. They do not rise as high as breads made with bread flour or all-purpose flour because whole wheat flour has less protein. For better volume, use half whole wheat flour with half bread flour.

Whole wheat blend flour: This combination of whole wheat and unbleached flours gives the performance of all-purpose with the added nutritional benefits of whole wheat. You can use it cup for cup, instead of all-purpose flour, for a yeast bread that's lighter than a bread made entirely of whole wheat flour.

Quick-mixing flour: An enriched all-purpose flour in a granular form that blends very readily with liquid and is used primarily to make gravies and sauces and to thicken main dishes. It has the same characteristics as all-purpose flour. It is not recommended for bread machines because of lower protein than bread flour.

Self-rising flour: A convenience flour that includes leavening ingredients and salt. Typically used for light and fluffy biscuits and tender cakes, it is not recommended for bread machines because the chemical leavening and additional salt compete with the yeast.

Cake flour: A flour milled from soft wheats lower in gluten-forming protein than all-purpose flour. It's ideal for cakes, resulting in a tender crumb and fine texture. It is not recommended for bread machines because of the low amount of protein.

Rye flour: Milled from rye grain instead of wheat. This flour is usually combined with wheat flour for bread making to increase the dough's gluten-forming capabilities, producing a dough with greater elasticity and better volume.

Yeast: A live plant that is the essence of yeast bread. When activated by warm liquid and fed by sugar or starch, yeast releases tiny bubbles of carbon dioxide gas, makeing dough rise. For best results, yeast needs adequate amounts of liquid (at the right temperature) and other bread ingredients. Also, check the expiration date of the yeast before using. There are four types of yeast: *bread machine, quick active dry, regular active dry* and *compressed cake. Bread machine* yeast is a special strain of instant yeast. Its finer granulation means the yeast is dispersed more thoroughly during mixing and kneading. The result is a better loaf of bread. If a recipe calls for quick or regular active dry yeast, you may substitute the same amount of bread machine yeast. If the results do not meet your expectations, try decreasing the amount of bread machine yeast by 1/4 teaspoon. *Quick* and *regular active dry* yeast can be used in bread machines. However, *compressed cake* yeast is generally not used in bread machines because it is difficult to measure.

Sweeteners: Provide food for yeast to work. Sweeteners, including sugar, honey and molasses, also add flavor and help the crust brown. Artificial sweeteners are not recommended for yeast baking because they do not feed the yeast like regular sweeteners do.

Salt: Controls yeast growth to prevent overrising, which can cause the bread to collapse. Salt also adds flavor to breads.

Fat: Such as shortening, margarine, butter or oil, adds tenderness and flavor to breads.

Liquids: Such as water and milk are used rehydrate and activate the yeast and blend the flour to make a sticky, elastic dough. Use liquids at room temperature (70° to 80°). Water gives bread a crisper crust; milk gives bread a velvety texture and added nutrients. Do not use delay cycles with recipes that contain fresh milk because the milk can spoil and possibly cause bacteria growth and food poisoning.

Nonfat dry milk (in dry form): Often is used in bread machine recipes so the delay cycles can be used. If nonfat dry milk is not available, fresh milk may be substituted for the amount of water specified (and omit the water).

Eggs: Sometimes added to bread doughs for taste, richness and color. Use large eggs in recipes that call for eggs. Do not use delay cycles with recipes that contain eggs because the eggs can spoil and possibly cause bacteria growth and food poisoning. Egg washes, which can be either beaten egg, egg whites or a mixture of water and egg, can be brushed over bread dough before baking to give the bread a beautiful golden crust.

Guide to Great Bread

Your bread machine occasionally may produce a loaf that might not meet your expectations. Since each bread machine works a little differently, you may wish to try slight ingredient adjustments to improve results. Remember that it is very important to measure all ingredients carefully. Short, heavier loaves are to be expected when whole grains, whole-grain flours or all-purpose flour is substituted due to less protein.

We have listed unsatisfactory characteristics, possible causes and solutions. To pinpoint a problem, *choose only one change at a time,* rather than trying several different changes at once. Increase or decrease an ingredient by the amount listed and note the result.

LOAF DIDN'T RISE

Cause	Solution
Too much salt, which can inhibit yeast action	Decrease salt by 1/4 teaspoon
Too little sugar, which can inhibit rising	Increase sugar by 1 teaspoon
Too little fat, which can inhibit rising	Increase fat by 1 teaspoon
Old or improperly stored yeast	Check date of yeast
Delay cycle used	Do not use delay cycle
Ingredients placed in pan incorrectly	Place ingredients in pan as directed

MUSHROOM-SHAPED TOP

Cause	Solution
Too much yeast causing too much rising	Decrease yeast by 1/4 teaspoon
Too much sugar causing too much rising	Decrease sugar by 1 teaspoon
Too little salt causing too much rising	Increase salt by 1/4 teaspoon
Too much liquid	Decrease liquid by 1 tablespoon
Too much sugary ingredients (applesauce, raisins candied fruit, etc.)	Decrease by 1 tablespoon

LOAF IS TOO BROWN

Cause	Solution
Too much sugar, causing excess browning	Decrease sugar by 1 teaspoon
Too much fat, causing excess browning	Decrease fat by 1 teaspoon
Dark setting, causing excess browning	Try using a light-crust setting

LOAF COLLAPSED

Cause	Solution
Too much yeast, causing too much rising	Decrease yeast by 1/4 teaspoon
Too much sugar causing too much rising	Decrease sugar by 1 teaspoon
Too little salt causing too much rising	Increase salt by 1/4 teaspoon
Too much liquid	Decrease liquid by 1 tablespoon
Too many ingredients	Use correct size recipe for correct size of pan
Opening machine during rising and baking	Do not open machine
Hot and humid weather	Bake during coolest part of day and use refrigerated liquid; do not use delay cycles
Leaving baked loaf in machine	Remove loaf from machine and pan immediately after baking cycle is complete

LOAF IS HEAVY AND DRY

Cause	Solution
Too much flour	Decrease flour by 1 tablespoon
Too little liquid	Increase liquid by 1 tablespoon
Too little yeast	Increase yeast by 1/4 teaspoon

LOAF IS UNDERBAKED OR GUMMY IN THE CENTER

Cause	Solution
Too much flour, causing an underbaked loaf	Decrease flour by 1 tablespoon
Too much liquid or moist ingredients (bananas, applesauce, yogurt etc.)	Decrease liquid by 1 tablespoon

LOAF IS DIFFICULT TO SLICE

Cause	Solution
Too much liquid, causing it to be crumbly	Decrease liquid by 1 tablespoon

LOAF HAS A YEASTY AROMA OR COARSE TEXTURE OR IS OVERRISEN

Cause	Solution
Too much yeast	Decrease yeast by 1/4 teaspoon
Salt was omitted	Measure and add ingredients carefully

Cutting Bread Machine Loaves

Because loaves baked in a bread machine are shaped differently than traditional bread loaves, there are several ways to cut them:

- Use an electric knife for best results when cutting warm bread loaves. Otherwise, a sharp serrated or sawtooth bread knife works well.

- For square slices, place the loaf on its side and slice across the loaf. We find this the easiest way to cut loaves.

- For rectangular slices, place the loaf upright and cut from the top down. Slices may be cut in half, lengthwise or crosswise.

- For wedges, place the loaf upright and cut through to the center from the top down into wedges. Or cut loaf in half from the top down, then place *each half* cut side down and cut lengthwise into four, six or eight wedges.

- For other interesting shapes, use your imagination! Bread slices can be cut into triangles, finger-like strips, chunks or other interesting shapes using cookie cutters. Look for these ideas in the photographs throughout the book.

Storing Bread Machine Loaves

If you have leftover bread machine bread, store it as follows:

- Store bread tightly covered at room temperature up to three days. If weather is hot and humid, store in the freezer.

- Store bread tightly covered in the freezer up to two months. Slice the loaves before freezing, so using one slice at a time will be easy.

- Do not store bread machine bread in the refrigerator because it tends to dry out and become stale more quickly than commercially made bread.

- Leftover bread can be used in your favorite bread pudding, crouton and stuffing recipes. Keep a tightly closed container in the freezer to add to as needed.

How to Use Nutritional Information

Nutrition Information per serving for each recipe includes the amounts of calories, protein, carbohydrate, fat, cholesterol and sodium.

- If ingredient choices are given, the first listed ingredient is used in recipe nutrition information calculations.

- When ingredient ranges or more than one serving size is indicated, the first weight or serving is used to calculate nutrition information.

- "If desired" ingredients and recipe variations are not included in nutrition information calculations.

Breads for Every Occasion

Italian Night Out

Favorite Cheese Pizza (p. 64)
Savory Calzones (p. 70)
Parmesan-Garlic Twists (p. 70)
Italian Parmesan Butter (p. 81)

Breakfast Bar

Sally Lunn (p. 14)
Raised Doughnuts (p. 78)
Glazed Cinnamon Rolls (p. 79)
Spicy Apple Bread (p. 48)

Viva la France!

French Baguettes (p. 59)
Miniature Brioche (p. 70)
French Twists (p. 72)
French Onion Tart (p. 60)

South-of-the-Border Surprise

Salsa Bread (p. 25)
Taco-Cheddar Bread (p. 29)
Jalapeño Corn Bread (p. 45)
Savory Roasted Pepper Bread (p. 24)

Gifts for Giving

Challah Braid (p. 62)
Coffee-Amaretto Bread (p. 56)
Coconut-Pecan Braid (p. 74)
Banana–Chocolate Chip Bread (p. 50)
Panettone (p. 53)

Coffee Break

Fruited Coffee Cake (p. 76)
Caramel-Pecan Rolls (p. 74)
Cinnamon-Raisin Bread (p. 15)
Crunchy Applesauce Bread (p. 48)
Almond–Chocolate Chip Bread (p. 54)

Housewarming Cheer

Fireside Cheddar-Olive Bread (p. 27)
Pesto-Tomato Bread (p. 30)
Fresh Herb Bread (p. 33)
Cherry-Almond Loaf (p. 54)
Blueberry-Lemon Loaf (p. 51)

Honey-Sunflower Loaf (p.35)

1

Classic and Savory Loaves

Classic White Bread

1-Pound Recipe (8 slices)		1 1/2-Pound Recipe (12 slices)
3/4 cup plus 1 tablespoon	Water	1 cup plus 2 tablespoons
1 tablespoon	Margarine or butter, softened	2 tablespoons
2 cups	Bread flour	3 cups
2 tablespoons	Dry milk	3 tablespoons
1 tablespoon	Sugar	2 tablespoons
1 teaspoon	Salt	1 1/2 teaspoons
1 1/4 teaspoons	Bread machine yeast	2 teaspoons

Make 1 1/2-Pound Recipe for bread machines that use 3 cups flour, or make 1-Pound Recipe for bread machines that use 2 cups flour.

Measure all ingredients carefully and place in bread machine pan in the order recommended by the manufacturer.

Select Basic/White cycle. Use Medium or Light crust color. Remove baked bread from pan and cool on wire rack.

Serving Size: 1 Slice Calories 145 (Calories from Fat 20) Fat 2g (Saturated 1g); Cholesterol 0mg; Sodium 300mg; Carbohydrate 29g; (Dietary Fiber 1g); Protein 4g

Buttermilk Bread

1-Pound Recipe (8 slices)		1 1/2-Pound Recipe (12 slices)
3/4 cup plus 2 tablespoons	Buttermilk	1 1/4 cups
2 tablespoons	Margarine or butter, softened	3 tablespoons
2 tablespoons	Honey	3 tablespoons
2 1/2 cups	Bread flour	3 1/4 cups
1 teaspoon	Salt	1 1/2 teaspoons
1/4 teaspoon	Baking soda	1/4 teaspoon
1 teaspoon	Bread machine yeast	1 1/2 teaspoons

Make 1 1/2-Pound Recipe with bread machines that use 3 cups flour, or make 1-Pound Recipe with bread machines that use 2 cups flour.

Measure carefully, placing all ingredients in bread machine pan in the order recommended by the manufacturer.

Select Basic/White cycle. Use Medium or Light crust color. Do not use delay cycles. Remove baked bread from pan and cool on wire rack.

Serving Size: 1 Slice Calories 180 (Calories from Fat 25); Fat 3g (Saturated 1g); Cholesterol 0mg; Sodium 350mg; Carbohydrate 34g; (Dietary Fiber 1g); Protein 5g

Sally Lunn

This popular tea bread is believed to have been named for a woman who worked in the bakery where it was created.

1 Pound Recipe (8 slices)		1 1/2-Pound Recipe (12 slices)
1 egg plus enough water to measure 3/4 cup	Egg	1 egg plus enough water to measure 1 cup plus 2 tablespoons
3/4 teaspoon	Salt	1 teaspoon
1 tablespoon	Sugar	1 tablespoon plus 1 teaspoon
1/4 cup (1/2 stick)	Butter, softened*	1/4 cup (1/2 stick) plus 2 tablespoons
2 cups	Bread flour	3 cups
3/4 teaspoon	Bread machine yeast	1 teaspoon

Make 1 1/2-Pound Recipe with bread machines that use 3 cups flour, or make 1-Pound Recipe with bread machines that use 2 cups flour.

Measure carefully, placing all ingredients in bread machine pan in the order recommended by the manufacturer.

Select Sweet or Basic/White cycle. Use Medium or Light crust color. Do not use delay cycles. Remove baked bread from pan and cool on wire rack.

*We do not recommend margarine for this recipe.

Serving Size: 1 Slice Calories 185 (Calories from Fat 65); Fat 7g (Saturated 4g); Cholesterol 35mg; Sodium 220mg; Carbohydrate 28g; (Dietary Fiber 1g); Protein 4g

Cinnamon-Raisin Bread

This bread is perfect in the morning with your favorite spread or as a late-night treat when you're looking for something not-too-sweet.

1-Pound Recipe (8 slices)		1 1/2-Pound Recipe (12 slices)
3/4 cup plus 1 tablespoon	Water	1 cup plus 2 tablespoons
1 tablespoon	Margarine or butter, softened	2 tablespoons
2 cups	Bread flour	3 cups
2 tablespoons	Sugar	3 tablespoons
1 teaspoon	Salt	1 1/2 teaspoons
3/4 teaspoon	Ground cinnamon	1 teaspoon
1 1/2 teaspoons	Bread machine yeast	2 1/2 teaspoons
1/2 cup	Raisins	3/4 cup

Make 1 1/2-Pound Recipe with bread machines that use 3 cups flour, or make 1-Pound Recipe with bread machines that use 2 cups flour.

Measure carefully, placing all ingredients except raisins in bread machine pan in the order recommended by the manufacturer. Add raisins at the Raisin/Nut signal or 5 to 10 minutes before last kneading cycle ends.

Select Sweet or Basic/White cycle. Use Medium or Light crust color. Remove baked bread from pan and cool on wire rack.

Serving Size: 1 Serving Calories 175 (Calories from Fat 20); Fat 2g (Saturated 1g); Cholesterol 0mg; Sodium 290mg; Carbohydrate 37g; (Dietary Fiber 2g); Protein 4g

Ranch Bread

1-Pound Recipe (8 slices)		1 1/2-Pound Recipe (12 slices)
2/3 cup	Water	3/4 cup plus 2 tablespoons
1/4 cup	Bottled ranch-style dressing	1/3 cup
2 cups	Bread flour	3 cups
1 tablespoon	Sugar	2 tablespoons
3/4 teaspoon	Salt	1 teaspoon
1 1/4 teaspoons	Bread machine yeast	1 3/4 teaspoons

Make 1 1/2-Pound Recipe with bread machines that use 3 cups flour, or make 1-Pound Recipe with bread machines that use 2 cups flour.

Measure carefully, placing all ingredients in bread machine pan in the order recommended by the manufacturer.

Select Basic/White cycle. Use Medium or Light crust color. Do not use delay cycles. Remove baked bread from pan and cool on wire rack.

Serving Size: 1 Slice Calories 155 (Calories from Fat 25); Fat 3g (Saturated 1g); Cholesterol 2mg; Sodium 230mg; Carbohydrate 29g; (Dietary Fiber 1g); Protein 4g

Peanut Butter Bread

You'll go ape over a grilled peanut butter–banana sandwich! Construct it like a grilled cheese, only substitute peanut butter for the cheese and add a sliced banana. You'll have a toasted, gooey treat that goes down well with a glass of cold milk.

1-Pound Recipe (8 slices)		1 1/2-Pound Recipe (12 slices)
2/3 cup	Water	1 cup plus 1 tablespoon
1/4 cup	Peanut Butter	1/2 cup
2 cups	Bread flour	3 cups
2 tablespoons	Packed brown sugar	3 tablespoons
3/4 teaspoon	Salt	1 teaspoon
1 1/4 teaspoons	Bread machine yeast	2 teaspoons

Make 1 1/2-Pound Recipe with bread machines that use 3 cups flour, or make 1-Pound Recipe with bread machines that use 2 cups flour.

Measure carefully, placing all ingredients in bread machine pan in the order recommended by the manufacturer.

Select Sweet or Basic/White cycle. Use Medium or Light crust color. Remove baked bread from pan and cool on wire rack.

Serving Size: 1 Slice Calories 200 (Calories from Fat 55); Fat 6g (Saturated 1g); Cholesterol 0mg; Sodium 230mg; Carbohydrate 32g; (Dietary Fiber 2g); Protein 6g

---

Sandwich Savvy

The definition of a sandwich varies with the person you ask and is not restricted to a filling between two pieces of bread. The versatile sandwich can be served hot, cold, grilled, baked, fried, layered, stacked, rolled or open-faced and can be eaten with a knife and fork, cut in half or quartered.

Early Morning Pick-Me-Up: Spread toasted Cinnamon-Raisin Bread (p. 15) with creamy peanut butter, sliced banana and honey drizzled on top.

Southern Delight: Spread Praline Sweet Potato Bread (p. 34) with Curried Chutney Spread (p. 84) and then top with ham, thinly sliced apples and alfalfa sprouts.

Midwest Favorite: Spread Honey-Sunflower Loaf (p. 35) with honey-mustard and top with smoked turkey and coleslaw.

Thanksgiving Treat: Top toasted Buttermilk Bread (p. 14) with sliced turkey breast, cranberry sauce and leftover stuffing dressed with warmed gravy.

Octoberfest Fare: Top Sauerkraut-Rye Loaf (p. 42) with sliced cooked kielbasa, warm sauerkraut and spicy mustard.

Open-faced Veggie Feast: Layer Pumpkin–Whole Wheat Bread (p. 41) with thinly sliced avocado, tomato, lettuce, cucumber and Swiss cheese. Try warming it under the broiler for a minute or two to melt the cheese.

Double Mustard–Beer Bread

To make beer flat, just measure and let stand about 1 hour before using.

1-Pound Recipe (8 slices)		1 1/2-Pound Recipe (12 slices)
1/2 cup	Flat beer	3/4 cup
1/4 cup	Water	1/3 cup
3 tablespoons	Chopped onion	1/4 cup
1 tablespoon	Prepared mustard	2 tablespoons
2 teaspoons	Margarine or butter, softened	1 tablespoon
2 cups	Bread flour	3 cups
2 teaspoons	Sugar	1 tablespoon
1/2 teaspoon	Ground mustard	1 teaspoon
1/2 teaspoon	Salt	3/4 teaspoon
1 1/4 teaspoons	Bread machine yeast	1 3/4 teaspoons

Make 1 1/2-Pound Recipe with bread machines that use 3 cups flour, or make 1-Pound Recipe with bread machines that use 2 cups flour.

Measure carefully, placing all ingredients in bread machine pan in the order recommended by the manufacturer.

Select Basic/White cycle. Use Medium or Light crust color. Remove baked bread from pan and cool on wire rack.

Serving Size: 1 Slice Calories 135 (Calories from Fat 10); Fat 1g (Saturated 0g); Cholesterol 0mg; Sodium 180mg; Carbohydrate 28g; (Dietary Fiber 1g); Protein 4g

Dijon-Thyme Bread

1-Pound Recipe (8 slices)		1 1/2-Pound Recipe (12 slices)
2/3 cup	Water	1 cup
2 tablespoons	Dijon mustard	3 tablespoons
2 teaspoons	Vegetable oil	1 tablespoon
2 cups	Bread flour	3 cups
1 tablespoon	Sugar	2 tablespoons
1/2 teaspoon	Salt	3/4 teaspoon
1/2 teaspoon	Dried thyme leaves	1 teaspoon
1 1/4 teaspoons	Bread machine yeast	2 teaspoons

Make 1 1/2-Pound Recipe with bread machines that use 3 cups flour, or make 1-Pound Recipe with bread machines that use 2 cups flour.

Measure carefully, placing all ingredients in bread machine pan in the order recommended by the manufacturer.

Select Basic/White cycle. Use Medium or Light crust color. Remove baked bread from pan and cool on wire rack.

Serving Size: 1 Slice Calories 145 (Calories from Fat 20); Fat 2g (Saturated 0g); Cholesterol 0mg; Sodium 180mg; Carbohydrate 29g; (Dietary Fiber 1g); Protein 4g

Harvest Loaf

Dehydrated soup greens can be found in jars in the spice section of your supermarket.

1-Pound Recipe (8 slices)		1 1/2-Pound Recipe (12 slices)
3/4 cup	Water	1 cup plus 2 tablespoons
2 teaspoons	Margarine or butter, softened	1 tablespoon
2 cups	Bread flour	3 cups
2 tablespoons	Dehydrated soup greens	1/4 cup
1 tablespoon	Dry milk	2 tablespoons
1 tablespoon	Sugar	2 tablespoons
1 teaspoon	Salt	1 1/2 teaspoons
1/8 teaspoon	Garlic powder	1/4 teaspoon
1 1/2 teaspoons	Bread machine yeast	2 teaspoons

Make 1 1/2-Pound Recipe with bread machines that use 3 cups flour, or make 1-Pound Recipe with bread machines that use 2 cups flour.

Measure carefully, placing all ingredients in bread machine pan in the order recommended by the manufacturer.

Select Basic/White cycle. Use Medium or Light crust color. Remove baked bread from pan and cool on wire rack.

Serving Size: 1 Slice Calories 135 (Calories from Fat 10); Fat 1g (Saturated 0g); Cholesterol 0mg; Sodium 280mg; Carbohydrate 29g; (Dietary Fiber 1g); Protein 4g

Terrific Tops

Sprinkle these crumb toppings over hot cooked vegetables, creamed vegetables, casseroles or whatever else that might need a crunchy top.

Bread Topping: Mix 1/4 cup Classic White Bread (p. 13), Harvest Loaf (above) or Multigrain Loaf (p. 47) dry bread crumbs, 1 1/2 teaspoons margarine or butter, melted, and dash of salt.

Corn Bread Topping: Mix 1/4 cup Jalapeño Corn Bread (p. 45) dry bread crumbs, 1 1/2 teaspoons margarine or butter, melted, and dash of salt.

Garlic Bread Topping: Mix 1/4 cup Garlic-Basil Bread (p. 27) or Roasted Garlic Bread (p. 32) dry bread crumbs, 1 1/2 teaspoons margarine or butter, melted, and 1/2 small clove garlic, crushed, and dash of salt.

Herb Bread Topping: Mix 1/4 cup Fresh Herb Bread (p. 33), Dilled Brown Rice Bread (p. 26), Cottage Dill Bread (p. 22) or Potato-Chive Bread (p. 20) dry bread crumbs, 1 1/2 teaspoons margarine or butter, melted, and 3/4 teaspoon chopped fresh or 1/4 teaspoon dried herb leaves and dash of salt.

Harvest Loaf, Sticky Orange-Almond Rolls (p. 77)

Pepperoni Pizza Bread

1-Pound Recipe (8 slices)		1 1/2-Pound Recipe (12 slices)
3/4 cup	Water	1 cup plus 2 tablespoons
2 cups	Bread flour	3 cups
1/4 cup	Shredded mozzarella cheese	1/3 cup
1 tablespoon	Sugar	2 tablespoons
1 teaspoon	Garlic salt	1 1/2 teaspoons
1 teaspoon	Dried oregano leaves	1 1/2 teaspoons
1 teaspoon	Bread machine yeast	1 3/4 teaspoons
1/2 cup	Sliced pepperoni	2/3 cup

Make 1 1/2-Pound Recipe with bread machines that use 3 cups flour, or make 1-Pound Recipe with bread machines that use 2 cups flour.

Measure carefully, placing all ingredients except pepperoni in bread machine pan in the order recommended by the manufacturer. Add pepperoni at the Raisin/Nut signal or 5 to 10 minutes before last kneading cycle ends. *25 MINS AFTER START PUT IN PEPPERONI*

Select Basic/White cycle. Use Medium or Light crust color. Do not use delay cycles. Remove baked bread from pan and cool on wire rack.

Note: We do not recommend this recipe for 1 1/2-pound bread machines with cast-aluminum pans in horizontal-loaf shape.

Serving Size: 1 Slice Calories 170 (Calories from Fat 35); Fat 4g (Saturated 2g); Cholesterol 5mg; Sodium 270mg; Carbohydrate 29g; (Dietary Fiber 1g); Protein 6g

Potato-Chive Bread

1-Pound Recipe (8 slices)		1 1/2-Pound Recipe (12 slices)
3/4 cup	Water	1 cup plus 2 tablespoons
1 tablespoon	Margarine or butter, softened	2 tablespoons
2 cups	Bread flour	3 cups
1/3 cup	Mashed potato mix (dry)	1/2 cup
2 tablespoons	Chopped fresh chives OR	1/4 cup
1 tablespoon	Freeze-dried chives	2 tablespoons
2 teaspoons	Sugar	1 tablespoon
1 teaspoon	Salt	1 1/2 teaspoons
1 3/4 teaspoons	Bread machine yeast	2 3/4 teaspoons

Make 1 1/2-Pound Recipe with bread machines that use 3 cups flour, or make 1-Pound Recipe with bread machines that use 2 cups flour.

Measure carefully, placing all ingredients in bread machine pan in the order recommended by the manufacturer.

Select Basic/White cycle. Use Medium or Light crust color. Do not use delay cycles. Remove baked bread from pan and cool on wire rack.

Serving Size: 1 Slice Calories 145 (Calories from Fat 20); Fat 2g (Saturated 1g); Cholesterol 0mg; Sodium 290mg; Carbohydrate 29g; (Dietary Fiber 1g); Protein 4g

Pepperoni Pizza Bread

Cottage Dill Bread

1-Pound Recipe (8 slices)		1 1/2-Pound Recipe (12 slices)
1/2 cup	Water	2/3 cup
1/2 cup	Small curd creamed cottage cheese	2/3 cup
1 tablespoon	Margarine or butter, softened	2 tablespoons
2 cups	Bread flour	3 cups
2 teaspoons	Sugar	1 tablespoon
2 teaspoons	Dry milk	1 tablespoon
2 teaspoons	Instant minced onion	1 tablespoon
2 teaspoons	Dill seed	1 tablespoon
3/4 teaspoon	Salt	1 teaspoon
1 teaspoon	Bread machine yeast	1 1/2 teaspoons

Make 1 1/2-Pound Recipe with bread machines that use 3 cups flour, or make 1-Pound Recipe with bread machines that use 2 cups flour.

Measure carefully, placing all ingredients in bread machine pan in the order recommended by the manufacturer.

Select Basic/White cycle. Use Medium or Light crust color. Do not use delay cycles. Remove baked bread from pan and cool on wire rack.

Note: We do not recommend this recipe for 1 1/2-pound bread machines with cast-aluminum pans in horizontal-loaf shape.

Serving Size: 1 Slice Calories 155 (Calories from Fat 25); Fat 3g (Saturated 1g); Cholesterol 2mg; Sodium 250mg; Carbohydrate 28g; (Dietary Fiber 1g); Protein 5g

Savory Cheese Loaf

1-Pound Recipe (8 slices)		1 1/2-Pound Recipe (12 slices)
3/4 cup	Water (lukewarm)	1 cup plus 2 tablespoons
2 cups	Bread flour	3 cups
1/4 cup	Grated Parmesan cheese	1/3 cup
1 1/2 tablespoons	Dry milk	2 tablespoons
1 1/2 tablespoons	Sugar	2 tablespoons
1 1/4 teaspoons	Italian seasoning	2 teaspoons
3/4 teaspoon	Salt	1 1/4 teaspoons
1 1/2 teaspoons	Bread machine yeast	2 teaspoons

Make 1 1/2-Pound Recipe with bread machines that use 3 cups flour, or make 1-Pound Recipe with bread machines that use 2 cups flour.

Measure carefully, placing all ingredients in bread machine pan in the order recommended by the manufacturer.

Select Basic/White cycle. Use Medium or Light crust color. Remove baked bread from pan and cool on wire rack.

Serving Size: 1 Slice Calories 140 (Calories from Fat 10); Fat 1g (Saturated 1g); Cholesterol 2mg; Sodium 270mg; Carbohydrate 29g; (Dietary Fiber 1g); Protein 5g

Cottage Dill Bread, Salsa Bread (p. 25)

Savory Roasted Pepper Bread

1-Pound Recipe (8 slices)		1 1/2-Pound Recipe (12 slices)
1/2 cup	Water	3/4 cup
3 tablespoons	Chopped roasted red bell peppers (from a jar)	1/4 cup
2 teaspoons	Margarine or butter, softened	1 tablespoon
1 clove	Garlic, crushed	2 cloves
2 cups	Bread flour	3 cups
2 tablespoons	Grated Parmesan cheese	3 tablespoons
1 tablespoon	Sugar	2 tablespoons
1 teaspoon	Salt	1 1/2 teaspoons
1 teaspoon	Dried basil leaves	1 1/2 teaspoons
1 1/4 teaspoons	Bread machine yeast	2 teaspoons

Make 1 1/2-Pound Recipe with bread machines that use 3 cups flour, or make 1-Pound Recipe with bread machines that use 2 cups flour.

Measure carefully, placing all ingredients in bread machine pan in the order recommended by the manufacturer.

Select Basic/White cycle. Use Medium or Light crust color. Do not use delay cycles. Remove baked bread from pan and cool on wire rack.

Serving Size: 1 Slice Calories 145 (Calories from Fat 2); Fat 1g (Saturated 2g); Cholesterol 0mg; Sodium 300mg; Carbohydrate 29g; (Dietary Fiber 1g); Protein 4g

Parmesan–Pine Nut Bread

1-Pound Recipe (8 slices)		1 1/2-Pound Recipe (12 slices)
3/4 cup plus 1 tablespoon	Water	1 cup plus 2 tablespoons
2 teaspoons	Olive oil	1 tablespoon
2 cups	Bread flour	3 cups
3 tablespoons	Grated Parmesan cheese	1/4 cup
1 tablespoon	Dry milk	2 tablespoons
1 tablespoon	Sugar	2 tablespoons
1 teaspoon	Salt	1 1/2 teaspoons
1 1/4 teaspoons	Bread machine yeast	2 teaspoons
2 tablespoons	Pine nuts	3 tablespoons

Make 1 1/2-Pound Recipe for bread machines that use 3 cups flour or 1-Pound Recipe for bread machines that use 2 cups flour.

Measure all ingredients except pine nuts carefully and place in bread machine pan in the order recommended by the manufacturer. Add pine nuts at the Raisin/Nut signal or 5 to 10 minutes before last kneading cycle ends.

Select Basic/White cycle. Use medium or light crust color. Remove baked bread from pan and cool on wire rack.

Serving Size: 1 Slice Calories 155 (Calories from Fat 25); Fat 3g (Saturated 1g); Cholesterol 2mg; Sodium 300mg; Carbohydrate 29g; (Dietary Fiber 2g); Protein 5g

Salsa Bread

Cheddar-Corn Spread (p. 82) adds a great Mexican flair to this bread. Try it at your next fiesta!

1-Pound Recipe (8 slices)		1 1/2-Pound Recipe (12 slices)
1/2 cup	Prepared salsa	3/4 cup
1/4 cup	Water	1/3 cup plus 1 tablespoon
1 tablespoon	Margarine or butter, softened	2 tablespoons
2 cups	Bread flour	3 cups
1 tablespoon	Chopped fresh cilantro	2 tablespoons
1 tablespoon	Sugar	2 tablespoons
1 teaspoon	Salt	1 1/2 teaspoons
1 1/4 teaspoons	Bread machine yeast	2 teaspoons

Make 1 1/2-Pound Recipe with bread machines that use 3 cups flour, or make 1-Pound Recipe with bread machines that use 2 cups flour.

Measure carefully, placing all ingredients in bread machine pan in the order recommended by the manufacturer.

Select Basic/White cycle. Use Medium or Light crust color. Remove baked bread from pan and cool on wire rack.

Serving Size: 1 Slice Calories 145 (Calories from Fat 20); Fat 2g (Saturated 0g); Cholesterol 0mg; Sodium 390mg; Carbohydrate 30g; (Dietary Fiber 2g); Protein 4g

Cajun Bread

1-Pound Recipe (8 slices)		1 1/2-Pound Recipe (12 slices)
1/2 cup	Water	3/4 cup
1/4 cup	Chopped onion	1/3 cup
1/4 cup	Chopped green bell pepper	1/3 cup
1 clove	Garlic, finely chopped	1 clove
2 teaspoons	Margarine or butter, softened	1 tablespoon
2 cups	Bread flour	3 cups
1 tablespoon	Sugar	2 tablespoons
1 teaspoon	Cajun or Creole seasoning	2 teaspoons
3/4 teaspoon	Salt	1 1/4 teaspoons
1 teaspoon	Bread machine yeast	1 3/4 teaspoons

Make 1 1/2-Pound Recipe with bread machines that use 3 cups flour, or make 1-Pound Recipe with bread machines that use 2 cups flour.

Measure carefully, placing all ingredients in bread machine pan in the order recommended by the manufacturer.

Select Basic/White cycle. Use Medium or Light crust color. Do not use delay cycles. Remove baked bread from pan and cool on wire rack.

Serving Size: 1 Slice Calories 125 (Calories from Fat 10); Fat 1g (Saturated 0g); Cholesterol 0mg; Sodium 230mg; Carbohydrate 27g; (Dietary Fiber 1g); Protein 3g

Dilled Brown Rice Bread

1-Pound Recipe (8 slices)		1 1/2-Pound Recipe (12 slices)
3/4 cup	Water	1 cup
1 tablespoon	Vegetable oil	2 tablespoons
1 tablespoon	Packed brown sugar	2 tablespoons
1 3/4 cups	Bread flour	2 1/4 cups
1/2 cup	Whole wheat flour	3/4 cup
1/2 cup	Cooked brown rice	3/4 cup
2 teaspoons chopped fresh	Dill weed OR	1 tablespoon chopped fresh
1/2 teaspoon dried	Dill weed	3/4 teaspoon dried
2 tablespoons	Dry milk	3 tablespoons
3/4 teaspoon	Salt	1 1/2 teaspoons
1 teaspoon	Bread machine yeast	1 1/2 teaspoons

Make 1 1/2-Pound Recipe with bread machines that use 3 cups flour, or make 1-Pound Recipe with bread machines that use 2 cups flour.

Measure carefully, placing all ingredients in bread machine pan in the order recommended by the manufacturer.

Select Whole Wheat or Basic/White cycle. Use Medium or Light crust color. Remove baked bread from pan and cool on wire rack.

Serving Size: 1 Slice Calories 159 (Calories from Fat 25); Fat 3g (Saturated 1g); Cholesterol 0mg; Sodium 270mg; Carbohydrate 31g; (Dietary Fiber 2g); Protein 4g

Trail Mix Bread

1-Pound Recipe (8 slices)		1 1/2-Pound Recipe (12 slices)
3/4 cup plus 2 tablespoons	Water	1 1/4 cups
1 tablespoon	Vegetable oil	2 tablespoons
2 cups	Bread flour	3 cups
1/2 cup	Trail mix	2/3 cup
2 tablespoons	Packed brown sugar	3 tablespoons
3/4 teaspoon	Salt	1 teaspoon
1 teaspoon	Bread machine yeast	1 1/2 teaspoons

Make 1 1/2-Pound Recipe with bread machines that use 3 cups flour, or make 1-Pound Recipe with bread machines that use 2 cups flour.

Measure carefully, placing all ingredients in bread machine pan in the order recommended by the manufacturer.

Select Sweet or Basic/White cycle. Use Medium or Light crust color. Remove baked bread from pan and cool on wire rack.

Serving Size: 1 Slice Calories 190 (Calories from Fat 45); Fat 5g (Saturated 1g); Cholesterol 0mg; Sodium 200mg; Carbohydrate 33g; (Dietary Fiber 2g); Protein 5g

Fireside Cheddar-Olive Bread

1-Pound Recipe (8 slices)		1 1/2-Pound Recipe (12 slices)
3/4 cup	Water	1 cup plus 2 tablespoons
2 cups	Bread flour	3 cups
3/4 cup (3 ounces)	Shredded sharp Cheddar cheese	1 1/4 cups (5 ounces)
1 tablespoon	Sugar	1 tablespoon plus 1 1/2 teaspoons
1/2 teaspoon	Salt	3/4 teaspoon
3/4 teaspoon	Bread machine yeast	1 1/4 teaspoons
1/2 cup	Small pimiento-stuffed olives, well-drained	3/4 cup

Make 1 1/2-Pound Recipe with bread machines that use 3 cups flour, or make 1-Pound Recipe with bread machines that use 2 cups flour.

Measure carefully, placing all ingredients except olives in bread machine pan in the order recommended by the manufacturer. Add olives at the Raisin/Nut signal or 5 to 10 minutes before last kneading cycle ends.

Select Basic/White cycle. Use Medium or Light crust color. Do not use delay cycles. Remove baked bread from pan and cool on wire rack.

Note: We do not recommend this recipe for 1 1/2-pound bread machines with cast-aluminum pans in horizontal-loaf shape.

Serving Size: **1 Slice** Calories 180 (Calories from Fat 45); Fat 5g (Saturated 3g); Cholesterol 10mg; Sodium 430mg; Carbohydrate 28g; (Dietary Fiber 1g); Protein 7g

Garlic-Basil Bread

1-Pound Recipe (8 slices)		1 1/2-Pound Recipe (12 slices)
3/4 cup	Water	1 cup plus 1 tablespoon
2 teaspoons	Margarine or butter, softened	1 tablespoon
1 clove	Garlic, finely chopped	2 cloves
2 cups	Bread flour	3 cups
1 tablespoon	Dry milk	2 tablespoons
1 tablespoon	Sugar	2 tablespoons
1 teaspoon	Salt	1 1/2 teaspoons
1 teaspoon	Dried basil leaves	1 1/2 teaspoons
1 1/2 teaspoons	Bread machine yeast	2 1/4 teaspoons

Make 1 1/2-Pound Recipe with bread machines that use 3 cups flour, or make 1-Pound Recipe with bread machines that use 2 cups flour.

Measure carefully, placing all ingredients in bread machine pan in the order recommended by the manufacturer.

Select Basic/White cycle. Use Medium or Light crust color. Remove baked bread from pan and cool on wire rack.

Serving Size: **1 Slice** Calories 135 (Calories from Fat 10); Fat 1g (Saturated 0g); Cholesterol 0mg; Sodium 290mg; Carbohydrate 29g; (Dietary Fiber 1g); Protein 4g

Cheddar-Onion Bread

1-Pound Recipe (8 slices)		1 1/2-Pound Recipe (12 slices)
2/3 cup	Water	1 cup
2 cups	Bread flour	3 cups
1/2 cup	Shredded Cheddar cheese	3/4 cup
1 tablespoon	Sugar	2 tablespoons
2 teaspoons	Dry milk	1 tablespoon
1 1/2 teaspoons	Instant minced onion	2 teaspoons
3/4 teaspoon	Salt	1 teaspoon
3/4 teaspoon	Bread machine yeast	1 1/4 teaspoons

Make 1 1/2-Pound Recipe for bread machines that use 3 cups flour or 1-Pound Recipe for bread machines that use 2 cups flour.

Measure all ingredients carefully and place in bread machine pan in the order recommended by the manufacturer.

Select Basic/White cycle. Use medium or light crust color. Do not use delay cycles. Remove baked bread from pan and cool on wire rack.

Note: We do not recommend this recipe for 1 1/2-pound bread machines with cast-aluminum pans in horizontal-loaf shape.

Serving Size: **1 Slice** Calories 160 (Calories from Fat 25); Fat 3g (Saturated 2g); Cholesterol 5mg; Sodium 220mg; Carbohydrate 29g; (Dietary Fiber 1g); Protein 5g

Onion–Poppy Seed Loaf

Try combining this bread, toasted, with Basil-Pepper Spread (p. 84). It is great for a snack, or you can cut the bread into quarters and serve it as hors d'oeuvres at your next party.

1-Pound Recipe (8 slices)		1 1/2-Pound Recipe (12 slices)
2/3 cup	Water	1 cup
1/3 cup	Chopped onion	1/2 cup
2 teaspoons	Margarine or butter, softened	1 tablespoon
2 cups	Bread flour	3 cups
1 tablespoon	Poppy seed	2 tablespoons
1 tablespoon	Sugar	2 tablespoons
2 teaspoons	Dry milk	1 tablespoon
1 teaspoon	Salt	1 1/2 teaspoons
3/4 teaspoon	Bread machine yeast	1 1/2 teaspoons

Make 1 1/2-Pound Recipe with bread machines that use 3 cups flour, or make 1-Pound Recipe with bread machines that use 2 cups flour.

Measure carefully, placing all ingredients in bread machine pan in the order recommended by the manufacturer.

Select Basic/White cycle. Use Medium or Light crust color. Remove baked bread from pan and cool on wire rack.

Serving Size: **1 Slice** Calories 150 (Calories from Fat 20); Fat 2g (Saturated 0g); Cholesterol 0mg; Sodium 280mg; Carbohydrate 30g; (Dietary Fiber 1g); Protein 4g

Taco-Cheddar Bread

1-Pound Recipe (8 slices)		1 1/2-Pound Recipe (12 slices)
3/4 cup	Water	1 cup plus 2 tablespoons
2 cups	Bread flour	3 cups
1/2 cup (2 ounces)	Shredded Cheddar cheese	1 cup (4 ounces)
2 teaspoons	Taco seasoning mix (dry)	1 tablespoon
1 1/2 teaspoons	Sugar	1 tablespoon
1/2 teaspoon	Salt	3/4 teaspoon
3/4 teaspoon	Bread machine yeast	1 1/2 teaspoons

Make 1 1/2-Pound Recipe with bread machines that use 3 cups flour, or make 1-Pound Recipe with bread machines that use 2 cups flour.

Measure carefully, placing all ingredients in bread machine pan in the order recommended by the manufacturer.

Select Basic/White cycle. Use Medium or Light crust color. Do not use delay cycles. Remove baked bread from pan and cool on wire rack.

Note: We do not recommend this recipe for 1 1/2-pound bread machines with cast-aluminum pans in horizontal-loaf shape.

Serving Size: 1 Slice Calories 170 (Calories from Fat 35); Fat 4g (Saturated 2g); Cholesterol 10mg; Sodium 230mg; Carbohydrate 28g; (Dietary Fiber 1g); Protein 6g

Greek Olive Bread

1-Pound Recipe (8 slices)		1 1/2-Pound Recipe (12 slices)
3/4 cup plus 1 tablespoon	Water	1 cup plus 2 tablespoons
2 teaspoons	Olive or vegetable oil	1 tablespoon
2 cups	Bread flour	3 cups
1 tablespoon	Sugar	2 tablespoons
1/2 teaspoon	Salt	1 teaspoon
3/4 teaspoon	Bread machine yeast	1 1/4 teaspoons
1/3 cup	Kalamata or ripe olives, pitted and coarsely chopped	1/2 cup

Make 1 1/2-Pound Recipe with bread machines that use 3 cups flour, or make 1-Pound Recipe with bread machines that use 2 cups flour.

Measure carefully, placing all ingredients except olives in bread machine pan in the order recommended by the manufacturer. Add olives at the Raisin/Nut signal or 5 to 10 minutes before last kneading cycle ends.

Select Basic/White cycle. Use Medium or Light crust color. Do not use delay cycles. Remove baked bread from pan and cool on wire rack.

Serving Size: 1 Slice Calories 145 (Calories from Fat 20); Fat 2g (Saturated 0g); Cholesterol 0mg; Sodium 230mg; Carbohydrate 29g; (Dietary Fiber 1g); Protein 4g

Pesto-Tomato Bread

The pesto adds a wonderful flavor to this bread. You can use any pesto you want, whether it is conveniently bought from the grocery store or you make it yourself with your favorite recipe. Either way, it's delicious!

1-Pound Recipe (8 slices)		1 1/2-Pound Recipe (12 slices)
1/4 cup	Coarsely chopped, softened* sun-dried tomatoes (not oil-packed)	1/3 cup
3/4 cup	Water	1 cup plus 2 tablespoons
1/4 cup	Pesto	1/3 cup
2 cups	Bread flour	3 cups
1 tablespoon	Sugar	2 tablespoons
1 teaspoon	Salt	1 1/2 teaspoons
3/4 teaspoon	Bread machine yeast	1 1/4 teaspoons

Make 1 1/2-Pound Recipe with bread machines that use 3 cups flour, or make 1-Pound Recipe with bread machines that use 2 cups flour.

Measure carefully, placing all ingredients in bread machine pan in the order recommended by the manufacturer.

Select Basic/White cycle. Use Medium or Light crust color. Do not use delay cycles. Remove baked bread from pan and cool on wire rack.

---

*Soak tomatoes in 1 cup very hot water about 10 minutes or until softened; drain.

Serving Size: 1 Slice Calories 175 (Calories from Fat 45); Fat 5g (Saturated 1g); Cholesterol 0mg; Sodium 320mg; Carbohydrate 30g; (Dietary Fiber 1g); Protein 4g

Pesto-Tomato Bread

Roasted Garlic Bread

It's easy to roast your own garlic for this bread. The garlic adds such a wonderful flavor, you'll want to make it again and again.

1-Pound Recipe (8 slices)		1 1/2-Pound Recipe (12 slices)
1 bulb	Roasted Garlic (below)	2 bulbs
2/3 cup	Water	1 cup plus 2 tablespoons
1 teaspoon	Olive or vegetable oil	1 tablespoon
2 cups	Bread flour	3 cups
1 tablespoon	Sugar	2 tablespoons
1/2 teaspoon	Salt	1 teaspoon
1 teaspoon	Bread machine yeast	1 1/4 teaspoons

Make 1 1/2-Pound Recipe with bread machines that use 3 cups flour, or make 1-Pound Recipe with bread machines that use 2 cups flour.

Prepare Roasted Garlic. After squeezing garlic out of cloves, mash garlic slightly to measure 2 tablespoons for 1-Pound Recipe, or 3 tablespoons for 1 1/2-Pound Recipe.

Measure carefully, placing all ingredients except Roasted Garlic in bread machine pan in the order recommended by the manufacturer. Add mashed garlic at the Raisin/Nut signal or 5 to 10 minutes before last kneading cycle ends.

Select Basic/White cycle. Use Medium or Light crust color. Do not use delay cycles. Remove baked bread from pan and cool on wire rack.

ROASTED GARLIC

Heat oven to 350°. Carefully peel away paperlike skin from around 1 or 2 garlic bulbs, leaving just enough to hold bulb intact. Trim top of garlic bulb about 1/2 inch to expose cloves. Place stem end down on 12-inch square of aluminum foil. Drizzle each bulb with 2 teaspoons olive or vegetable oil. Wrap securely in foil; place in pie plate or shallow baking pan. Bake 45 to 50 minutes or until garlic is tender when pierced with toothpick or fork. Cool slightly. Gently squeeze garlic out of cloves.

Note: A 1-ounce bulb of garlic, roasted, equals about 1 tablespoon mashed garlic; a 2-ounce bulb equals about 2 tablespoons mashed garlic.

Serving Size: 1 Slice Calories 135 (Calories from Fat 10); Fat 1g (Saturated 0g); Cholesterol 0mg; Sodium 180mg; Carbohydrate 29g; (Dietary Fiber 1g); Protein 4g

Fresh Herb Bread

1-Pound Recipe (8 slices)		1 1/2-Pound Recipe* (12 slices)
3/4 cup plus 1 tablespoon	Water	1 cup plus 2 tablespoons
1 tablespoon	Margarine or butter, softened	2 tablespoons
2 cups	Bread flour	3 cups
1 teaspoon	Chopped fresh sage leaves	2 teaspoons
2 teaspoons	Chopped fresh basil leaves	1 tablespoon
2 teaspoons	Chopped fresh oregano leaves	1 tablespoon
1 teaspoon	Chopped fresh thyme leaves	2 teaspoons
2 tablespoons	Chopped fresh parsley	1/4 cup
2 tablespoons	Dry milk	3 tablespoons
1 tablespoon	Sugar	2 tablespoons
3/4 teaspoon	Salt	1 teaspoon
1 teaspoon	Bread machine yeast	1 1/2 teaspoons

Make 1 1/2-Pound Recipe with bread machines that use 3 cups flour, or make 1-Pound Recipe with bread machines that use 2 cups flour.

Measure carefully, placing all ingredients in bread machine pan in the order recommended by the manufacturer.

Select Basic/White cycle. Use Medium or Light crust color. Remove baked bread from pan and cool on wire rack.

*We recommend using bread machines with 9-cup or larger bread pan for the 1 1/2-Pound Recipe.

Serving Size: 1 Slice Calories 145 (Calories from Fat 20); Fat 2g (Saturated 1g); Cholesterol 0mg; Sodium 210mg; Carbohydrate 29g; (Dietary Fiber 1g); Protein 4g

Praline Sweet Potato Bread

Although used interchangeably in cooking, sweet potatoes and yams are actually not the same. The sweet potato's skin and flesh are paler and somewhat drier than the darker orange yam's, and yams are noticeably sweeter than sweet potatoes.

1-Pound Recipe (8 slices)		1 1/2-Pound Recipe (12 slices)
1/2 cup	Canned vacuum-pack sweet potatoes, drained and mashed*	3/4 cup
1/3 cup plus 2 tablespoons	Water	2/3 cup
1 tablespoon	Margarine or butter, softened	1 tablespoon
2 cups	Bread flour	3 cups
1/3 cup	Pecan halves	1/2 cup
2 tablespoons	Packed brown sugar	3 tablespoons
1 teaspoon	Salt	1 1/2 teaspoons
1/4 teaspoon	Ground nutmeg	1/2 teaspoon
3/4 teaspoon	Bread machine yeast	1 teaspoon

Make 1 1/2-Pound Recipe with bread machines that use 3 cups flour, or make 1-Pound Recipe with bread machines that use 2 cups flour.

Measure carefully, placing all ingredients in bread machine pan in the order recommended by the manufacturer.

Select Sweet or Basic/White cycle. Use Medium or Light crust color. Remove baked bread from pan and cool on wire rack.

*We do not recommend sweet potatoes packed in syrup for this recipe.

Serving Size: 1 Slice Calories 180 (Calories from Fat 35); Fat 4g (Saturated 1g); Cholesterol 0mg; Sodium 290mg; Carbohydrate 34g; (Dietary Fiber 2g); Protein 4g

Honey-Sunflower Loaf

Toasted, salted sunflower nuts can be substituted for the raw sunflower nuts.

1-Pound Recipe (8 slices)		1 1/2-Pound Recipe (12 slices)
2/3 cup	Water	1 cup
2 tablespoons	Vegetable oil	2 tablespoons
1 tablespoon	Honey	2 tablespoons
2 1/4 cups	Bread flour	3 1/4 cups
1/3 cup	Sunflower nuts	1/2 cup
1 teaspoon	Salt	1 1/2 teaspoons
1 1/4 teaspoons	Bread machine yeast	2 teaspoons

Make 1 1/2-Pound Recipe with bread machines that use 3 cups flour, or make 1-Pound Recipe with bread machines that use 2 cups flour.

Measure carefully, placing all ingredients in bread machine pan in the order recommended by the manufacturer.

Select Basic/White cycle. Use Medium or Light crust color. Remove baked bread from pan and cool on wire rack.

Note: Sunflower nuts can be added at the Raisin/Nut signal or 5 to 10 minutes before last kneading cycle ends, if desired.

Serving Size: 1 Slice Calories 185 (Calories from Fat 45); Fat 5g (Saturated 1g); Cholesterol 0mg; Sodium 310mg; Carbohydrate 32g; (Dietary Fiber 2g); Protein 5g

Great Granola Bread

1-Pound Recipe (8 slices)		1 1/2-Pound Recipe (12 slices)
3/4 cup plus 2 tablespoons	Water	1 1/4 cups
1 tablespoon	Margarine or butter, softened	2 tablespoons
1 tablespoon	Packed brown sugar	2 tablespoons
2 cups	Bread flour	3 cups
1/2 cup	Granola	3/4 cup
1 tablespoon	Dry milk	2 tablespoons
3/4 teaspoon	Salt	1 teaspoon
1 teaspoon	Bread machine yeast	1 1/2 teaspoons

Make 1 1/2-Pound Recipe with bread machines that use 3 cups flour, or make 1-Pound Recipe with bread machines that use 2 cups flour.

Measure carefully, placing all ingredients in bread machine pan in the order recommended by the manufacturer.

Select Sweet or Basic/White cycle. Use Medium or Light crust color. Remove baked bread from pan and cool on wire rack.

Serving Size: 1 Slice Calories 180 (Calories from Fat 35); Fat 4g (Saturated 1g); Cholesterol 0mg; Sodium 210mg; Carbohydrate 33g; (Dietary Fiber 2g); Protein 5g

Spicy Apple Bread (p. 48), Banana–Chocolate Chip Bread (p. 50), Peanut Butter–Honey Spread (p. 86)

2

Special Grains and Sweet Loaves

Almond Honey–Whole Wheat Bread

1-Pound Recipe (8 slices)		1 1/2-Pound Recipe (12 slices)
2/3 cup	Water	1 cup plus 2 tablespoons
2 tablespoons	Honey	3 tablespoons
1 tablespoon	Margarine or butter, softened	2 tablespoons
1 cup	Bread flour	1 1/2 cups
1 cup	Whole wheat flour	1 1/2 cups
2 tablespoons	Toasted slivered almonds	1/4 cup
3/4 teaspoon	Salt	1 teaspoon
1 teaspoon	Bread machine yeast	1 1/2 teaspoons

Make 1 1/2-Pound Recipe with bread machines that use 3 cups flour, or make 1-Pound Recipe with bread machines that use 2 cups flour.

Measure carefully, placing all ingredients in bread machine pan in the order recommended by the manufacturer.

Select Whole Wheat or Basic/White cycle. Use Medium or Light crust color. Remove baked bread from pan and cool on wire rack.

Serving Size: 1 Slice Calories 160 (Calories from Fat 35); Fat 4g (Saturated 1g); Cholesterol 0mg; Sodium 200mg; Carbohydrate 29g; (Dietary Fiber 2g); Protein 4g

Orange–Whole Wheat Bread, Oatmeal-Pecan Loaf (p. 43)

Whole Wheat–Cranberry Bread

1-Pound Recipe (8 slices)		1 1/2-Pound Recipe (12 slices)
3/4 cup	Water	1 cup plus 2 tablespoons
2 tablespoons	Honey	1/4 cup
1 tablespoon	Margarine or butter, softened	2 tablespoons
1 1/4 cups	Bread flour	2 cups
3/4 cup	Whole wheat flour	1 1/4 cups
1 teaspoon	Salt	1 1/2 teaspoons
1/4 teaspoon	Ground mace	3/4 teaspoon
1 1/4 teaspoons	Bread machine yeast	2 teaspoons
1/3 cup	Dried cranberries or golden raisins	1/2 cup

Make 1 1/2-Pound Recipe with bread machines that use 3 cups flour, or make 1-Pound Recipe with bread machines that use 2 cups flour.

Measure carefully, placing all ingredients except cranberries in bread machine pan in the order recommended by the manufacturer. Add cranberries at the Raisin/Nut signal or 5 to 10 minutes before last kneading cycle ends.

Select Whole Wheat or Basic/White cycle. Use Medium or Light crust color. Remove baked bread from pan and cool on wire rack. Serve with Cranberry-Orange Butter (p. 82), if desired.

Serving Size: 1 Slice Calories 170 (Calories from Fat 20); Fat 2g (Saturated 0g); Cholesterol 0mg; Sodium 290mg; Carbohydrate 36g; (Dietary Fiber 2g); Protein 4g

Orange–Whole Wheat Bread

1-Pound Recipe (8 slices)		1 1/2-Pound Recipe (12 slices)
3/4 cup plus 1 tablespoon	Water	1 1/4 cups
1 tablespoon	Margarine or butter, softened	2 tablespoons
1 cup	Bread flour	1 1/2 cups
1 cup	Whole wheat flour	1 1/2 cups
2 tablespoons	Wheat germ	3 tablespoons
1 tablespoon	Dry milk	2 tablespoons
1 tablespoon	Sugar	2 tablespoons
1 teaspoon	Salt	1 1/2 teaspoons
1 teaspoon	Grated orange peel	1 1/2 teaspoons
1 1/4 teaspoons	Bread machine yeast	2 teaspoons

Make 1 1/2-Pound Recipe with bread machines that use 3 cups flour, or make 1-Pound Recipe with bread machines that use 2 cups flour.

Measure carefully, placing all ingredients in bread machine pan in the order recommended by the manufacturer.

Select Whole Wheat or Basic/White cycle. Use Medium or Light crust color. Remove baked bread from pan and cool on wire rack.

Serving Size: 1 Slice Calories 150 (Calories from Fat 25); Fat 3g (Saturated 1g); Cholesterol 0mg; Sodium 290mg; Carbohydrate 28g; (Dietary Fiber 2g); Protein 5g

Pumpkin–Whole Wheat Bread

Pumpkin–Whole Wheat Bread

1-Pound Recipe (8 slices)		1 1/2-Pound Recipe (12 slices)
1/2 cup	Canned pumpkin	3/4 cup
1/3 cup	Water	2/3 cup
1 tablespoon	Margarine or butter, softened	1 tablespoon
1 1/2 cups	Bread flour	2 cups
1/2 cup	Whole wheat flour	1 cup
2 tablespoons	Packed brown sugar	1/4 cup
1 teaspoon	Salt	1 1/2 teaspoons
1/2 teaspoon	Pumpkin pie spice	3/4 teaspoon
1 teaspoon	Bread machine yeast	1 3/4 teaspoons

Make 1 1/2-Pound Recipe with bread machines that use 3 cups flour, or make 1-Pound Recipe with bread machines that use 2 cups flour.

Measure carefully, placing all ingredients in bread machine pan in the order recommended by the manufacturer.

Select Sweet or Basic/White cycle. Use Medium or Light crust color. Remove baked bread from pan and cool on wire rack.

Serving Size: 1 Slice Calories 140 (Calories from Fat 10); Fat 1 (Saturated 0g); Cholesterol 0mg; Sodium 280mg; Carbohydrate 31g; (Dietary Fiber 2g); Protein 4g

Homemade Croutons

Cut bread (see p. 30) into 1/2-inch slices; spread one side with softened margarine or butter. Cut into 1/2-inch cubes. Sprinkle with chopped herbs, grated Parmesan cheese or spices, if desired. Place in ungreased heavy skillet. Cook over medium heat, stirring frequently, 4 to 7 minutes or until golden brown.

Caraway-Rye Bread

1-Pound Recipe (8 slices)		1 1/2-Pound Recipe (12 slices)
3/4 cup	Water	1 cup plus 3 tablespoons
2 teaspoons	Margarine or butter, softened	1 tablespoon
1 1/2 cups	Bread flour	2 1/2 cups
1/2 cup	Rye flour	3/4 cup
1 tablespoon	Dry milk	2 tablespoons
1 tablespoon	Sugar	2 tablespoons
1 teaspoon	Salt	1 1/2 teaspoons
1/8 teaspoon	Caraway seed	3/4 teaspoon
1 1/4 teaspoons	Bread machine yeast	2 1/4 teaspoons

Make 1 1/2-Pound Recipe with bread machines that use 3 cups flour, or make 1-Pound Recipe with bread machines that use 2 cups flour.

Measure carefully, placing all ingredients in bread machine pan in the order recommended by the manufacturer.

Select Basic/White cycle. Use Medium or Light crust color. Remove baked bread from pan and cool on wire rack.

Serving Size: 1 Slice Calories 135 (Calories from Fat 10); Fat 1g (Saturated 0g); Cholesterol 0mg; Sodium 280mg; Carbohydrate 29g; (Dietary Fiber 2g); Protein 4g

Sauerkraut-Rye Loaf

1-Pound Recipe (8 slices)		1 1/2-Pound Recipe (12 slices)
2/3 cup	Sauerkraut, well-drained	1 cup
1/2 cup plus 1 tablespoon	Water	3/4 cup
2 teaspoons	Molasses	1 tablespoon
2 teaspoons	Margarine or butter, softened	1 tablespoon
1 1/2 cups	Bread flour	2 1/4 cups
2/3 cup	Rye flour	1 cup
1 tablespoon	Packed brown sugar	2 tablespoons
3/4 teaspoon	Caraway seed	2 teaspoons
3/4 teaspoon	Salt	1 teaspoon
1 teaspoon	Bread machine yeast	1 1/2 teaspoons

Make 1 1/2-Pound Recipe with bread machines that use 3 cups flour, or make 1-Pound Recipe with bread machines that use 2 cups flour.

Measure carefully, placing all ingredients in bread machine pan in the order recommended by the manufacturer.

Select Basic/White or Whole Wheat cycle. Use Medium crust color. Do not use delay cycles. Remove baked bread from pan and cool on wire rack.

Serving Size: 1 Slice Calories 135 (Calories from Fat 10); Fat 1g (Saturated 0g); Cholesterol 0mg; Sodium 320mg; Carbohydrate 31g; (Dietary Fiber 3g); Protein 4g

Currant-Oatmeal Bread

Currants are smaller and a little sweeter than raisins. If you like, raisins can be substituted, measure for measure, for currants.

1-Pound Recipe (8 slices)		1 1/2-Pound Recipe (12 slices)
3/4 cup plus 2 tablespoons	Water	1 1/4 cups
1 tablespoon	Margarine or butter, softened	2 tablespoons
2 cups	Bread flour	3 cups
1/3 cup	Old-fashioned oats	1/2 cup
1/3 cup	Currants or raisins	1/2 cup
2 tablespoons	Packed brown sugar	3 tablespoons
1 tablespoon	Dry milk	2 tablespoons
3/4 teaspoon	Salt	1 1/4 teaspoons
3/4 teaspoon	Ground cinnamon	1 teaspoon
1 1/2 teaspoons	Bread machine yeast	2 teaspoons

Make 1 1/2-Pound Recipe with bread machines that use 3 cups flour, or make 1-Pound Recipe with bread machines that use 2 cups flour.

Measure carefully, placing all ingredients in bread machine pan in the order recommended by the manufacturer.

Select Sweet or Basic/White cycle. Use Medium or Light crust color. Remove baked bread from pan and cool on wire rack.

Serving Size: 1 Slice Calories 185 (Calories from Fat 25); Fat 3g (Saturated 1g); Cholesterol 0mg; Sodium 250mg; Carbohydrate 37g; (Dietary Fiber 2g); Protein 5g

Oatmeal-Pecan Loaf

1-Pound Recipe (8 slices)		1 1/2-Pound Recipe (12 slices)
3/4 cup plus 2 tablespoons	Water	1 1/4 cups
1 tablespoon	Margarine or butter, softened	2 tablespoons
2 cups	Bread flour	3 cups
1/3 cup	Old-fashioned oats	1/2 cup
1/3 cup	Chopped pecans	1/2 cup
2 tablespoons	Sugar	3 tablespoons
1 tablespoon	Dry milk	2 tablespoons
3/4 teaspoon	Salt	1 1/4 teaspoons
1 1/4 teaspoons	Bread machine yeast	2 teaspoons

Make 1 1/2-Pound Recipe with bread machines that use 3 cups flour, or make 1-Pound Recipe with bread machines that use 2 cups flour.

Measure carefully, placing all ingredients in bread machine pan in the order recommended by the manufacturer.

Select Sweet or Basic/White cycle. Use Medium or Light crust color. Remove baked bread from pan and cool on wire rack.

Serving Size: 1 Slice Calories 200 (Calories from Fat 55); Fat 6g (Saturated 1g); Cholesterol 0mg; Sodium 250mg; Carbohydrate 33g; (Dietary Fiber 2g); Protein 5g

Jalapeño Corn Bread, Cheddar-Corn Spread (p. 82)

Jalapeño Corn Bread

1-Pound Recipe (8 slices)		**1 1/2-Pound Recipe** (12 slices)
1/2 cup	Water	3/4 cup plus 2 tablespoons
1/2 cup	Frozen whole kernel corn, thawed	2/3 cup
1 tablespoon	Margarine or butter, softened	2 tablespoons
2 teaspoons	Chopped jalapeño chile	1 tablespoon
2 cups	Bread flour	3 1/4 cups
1/4 cup	Cornmeal	1/3 cup
1 tablespoon	Sugar	2 tablespoons
1 teaspoon	Salt	1 1/2 teaspoons
1 1/2 teaspoons	Bread machine yeast	2 1/2 teaspoons

Make 1 1/2-Pound Recipe with bread machines that use 3 cups flour, or make 1-Pound Recipe with bread machines that use 2 cups flour.

Measure carefully, placing all ingredients in bread machine pan in the order recommended by the manufacturer.

Select Basic/White cycle. Use Medium or Light crust color. Do not use delay cycles. Remove baked bread from pan and cool on wire rack.

Note: We do not recommend this recipe for bread machines with glass-domed lids.

Serving Size: 1 Slice Calories 175 (Calories from Fat 20); Fat 2g (Saturated 1g); Cholesterol 0mg; Sodium 290mg; Carbohydrate 36g; (Dietary Fiber 2g); Protein 5g

Multigrain Loaf

Multigrain Loaf

Look for 7-grain cereal in the health food or hot cereal section of your supermarket.

1-Pound Recipe (8 slices)		1 1/2-Pound Recipe (12 slices)
3/4 cup plus 2 tablespoons	Water	1 1/4 cups
1 tablespoon	Margarine or butter, softened	2 tablespoons
1 cup	Bread flour	1 1/3 cups
3/4 cup	Whole wheat flour	1 1/3 cups
2/3 cup	7-grain cereal	1 cup
2 tablespoons	Packed brown sugar	3 tablespoons
1 teaspoon	Salt	1 1/4 teaspoons
2 teaspoons	Bread machine yeast	2 1/2 teaspoons

Make 1 1/2-Pound Recipe with bread machines that use 3 cups flour, or make 1-Pound Recipe with bread machines that use 2 cups flour.

Measure carefully, placing all ingredients in bread machine pan in the order recommended by the manufacturer.

Select Whole Wheat or Basic/White cycle. Use Medium or Light crust color. Remove baked bread from pan and cool on wire rack.

Serving Size: 1 Slice Calories 135 (Calories from Fat 20); Fat 2g (Saturated 1g); Cholesterol 0mg; Sodium 270mg; Carbohydrate 27g; (Dietary Fiber 2g); Protein 4g

Spicy Apple Bread

Apple Pie Spice can be made by mixing 2 parts cinnamon with 1 part nutmeg to equal the amount called for.

1-Pound Recipe (8 slices)		1 1/2-Pound Recipe (12 slices)
2/3 cup	Water	1 cup plus 1 tablespoon
1 tablespoon	Margarine or butter, softened	2 tablespoons
2 cups	Bread flour	3 cups
1/4 cup	Cut-up dried apples	1/3 cup
1 tablespoon	Dry milk	2 tablespoons
1 tablespoon	Sugar	2 tablespoons
1 teaspoon	Salt	1 1/2 teaspoons
1 1/2 teaspoons	Apple pie spice	2 1/2 teaspoons
1 1/2 teaspoons	Bread machine yeast	2 teaspoons

Make 1 1/2-Pound Recipe with bread machines that use 3 cups flour, or make 1-Pound Recipe with bread machines that use 2 cups flour.

Measure carefully, placing all ingredients in bread machine pan in the order recommended by the manufacturer.

Select Sweet or Basic/White cycle. Use Medium or Light crust color. Remove baked bread from pan and cool on wire rack.

Serving Size: 1 Slice Calories 155 (Calories from Fat 20); Fat 2g (Saturated 0g); Cholesterol 0mg; Sodium 300mg; Carbohydrate 31g; (Dietary Fiber 1g); Protein 4g

Crunchy Applesauce Bread

1-Pound Recipe (8 slices)		1 1/2-Pound Recipe (12 slices)
2/3 cup	Water	3/4 cup plus 2 tablespoons
1/4 cup	Unsweetened applesauce	1/3 cup
2 teaspoons	Margarine or butter, softened	1 tablespoon
2 cups	Bread flour	3 cups
1/4 cup	Cracked wheat	1/3 cup
1/4 cup	Chopped walnuts	1/3 cup
1 tablespoons	Brown sugar	2 tablespoons
1 teaspoon	Salt	1 1/2 teaspoons
1 teaspoon	Bread machine yeast	1 1/2 teaspoons

Make 1 1/2-Pound Recipe for bread machines that use 3 cups flour, or 1-Pound Recipe for bread machines that use 2 cups flour.

Measure all ingredients except walnuts carefully and place in bread machine pan in the order recommended by the manufacturer. Add walnuts at the Raisin/Nut signal or 5 to 10 minutes before last kneading cycle ends.

Select Basic/White or Sweet cycle. Do not use delay cycles. Use Medium or Light crust color.

Remove baked bread from pan and cool on wire rack.

Note: We do not recommend this recipe for bread machines with glass-domed lids.

Serving Size: 1 Slice Calories 160 (Calories from Fat 25); Fat 3g (Saturated 0g); Cholesterol 0mg; Sodium 280mg; Carbohydrate 30g; (Dietary Fiber 1g); Protein 4g

Double Apricot–Almond Bread

1-Pound Recipe (8 slices)		1 1/2-Pound Recipe (12 slices)
1/3 cup	Lukewarm water	1/2 cup
1 jar (4 ounces)	Apricot baby food (reserve 1 teaspoon)	1 jar (6 ounces)
1 tablespoon	Margarine or butter, softened	2 tablespoons
2 cups	Bread flour	3 cups
1 tablespoon	Dry milk	2 tablespoons
1 tablespoon	Sugar	2 tablespoons
1 teaspoon	Salt	1 1/2 teaspoons
1/8 to 1/4 teaspoon	Ground nutmeg	1/4 to 1/2 teaspoon
1 teaspoon	Bread machine yeast	2 teaspoons
1/3 cup	Quartered dried apricots	1/2 cup
1/3 cup	Coarsely chopped toasted almonds	1/2 cup
	Apricot Glaze (below)	

Make 1 1/2-Pound Recipe with bread machines that use 3 cups flour, or make 1-Pound Recipe with bread machines that use 2 cups flour.

Measure carefully, placing all ingredients except the 1 teaspoon reserved baby food, apricots, almonds and Apricot Glaze in bread machine pan in the order recommended by the manufacturer. Add apricots and almonds at the Raisin/Nut signal or 5 to 10 minutes before last kneading cycle ends.

Select Sweet or Basic/White cycle. Use Medium or Light crust color. Do not use delay cycles. Remove baked bread from pan and cool on wire rack. Prepare Apricot Glaze; drizzle onto cooled loaf.

APRICOT GLAZE

1/2 cup powdered sugar
1 teaspoon reserved apricot baby food
1 teaspoon milk
Dash of nutmeg

Mix all ingredients until smooth and thin enough to drizzle.

Serving Size: 1 Slice Calories 220 (Calories from Fat 45); Fat 5g (Saturated 1g); Cholesterol 0mg; Sodium 300mg; Carbohydrate 41g; (Dietary Fiber 2g); Protein 5g

Bread Crumb Bonanza

Bread Crumbs (dry): Place bread (see p. 50) in 200° oven until dry. Place dry bread in heavy plastic bag or between sheets of waxed paper. Crush with rolling pin or mallet into very small pieces. You can also place in blender or food processor to make fine bread crumbs.

Bread Crumbs (soft): Tear soft bread into small pieces.

Banana–Chocolate Chip Bread

1-Pound Recipe (8 slices)		1 1/2-Pound Recipe (12 slices)
1/2 cup	Water	2/3 cup
1/3 cup	Mashed ripe bananas	2/3 cup
1 tablespoon	Margarine or butter, softened	2 tablespoons
1 egg white	Egg	1 whole egg
2 cups	Bread flour	3 cups
2 tablespoons	Sugar	3 tablespoons
3/4 teaspoon	Salt	1 1/4 teaspoons
1 1/2 teaspoons	Bread machine yeast	2 1/4 teaspoons
1/3 cup	Miniature semisweet chocolate chips	1/2 cup

Make 1 1/2-Pound Recipe with bread machines that use 3 cups flour, or make 1-Pound Recipe with bread machines that use 2 cups flour.

Measure carefully, placing all ingredients except chocolate chips in bread machine pan in the order recommended by the manufacturer. Add chocolate chips at the Raisin/Nut signal or 5 to 10 minutes before last kneading cycle ends.

Select Sweet or Basic/White cycle. Use Medium or Light crust color. Do not use delay cycles. Remove baked bread from pan and cool on wire rack.

Note: Depending on ripeness of bananas, dough may require more flour than recipe recommends. Five minutes after cycle begins, check consistency of dough. If dough is not forming a ball and seems wet, add additional flour, 1 tablespoon at a time, until a soft dough forms.

Serving Size: 1 Slice Calories 205 (Calories from Fat 45); Fat 5g (Saturated 2g); Cholesterol 20mg; Sodium 250mg; Carbohydrate 37g; (Dietary Fiber 2g); Protein 5g

---

More than Basic Bread

Looking for ideas to use up leftover bread? Try using these tasty breads with your favorite recipes:

Crumbly Bread Toppings (p. 18): Cheddar-Onion Bread (p. 28), Savory Cheese Loaf (p. 22), Honey-Sunflower Loaf (p. 35), Pepperoni Pizza Bread (p. 20)

Oven Stuffing: Dijon-Thyme Bread (p. 17), Roasted Garlic Bread (p. 32), Praline Sweet Potato Bread (p. 34), Oatmeal-Pecan Loaf (p. 43), Jalapeño Corn Bread (p. 45), Dilled Brown Rice Bread (p. 26)

Bread Pudding: Classic White Bread (p. 13), Crunchy Applesauce Bread (p. 48), Pumpkin–Whole Wheat Bread (p. 41), Buttermilk Bread (p. 14), Cinnamon-Raisin Bread (p. 15)

Croutons (p. 41): Fresh Herb Bread (p. 33), Ranch Bread (p. 15), Potato-Chive Bread (p. 20), Savory Roasted Pepper Bread (p. 24), Greek Olive Bread (p. 29)

French Toast: Banana–Chocolate Chip Bread (above), Great Granola Bread (p. 35), Coffee-Amaretto Bread (p. 56), Challah Braid (p. 62), Currant-Oatmeal Bread (p. 43)

Blueberry-Lemon Loaf

For a special treat, spread with softened cream cheese.

1-Pound Recipe (8 slices)		1 1/2-Pound Recipe (12 slices)
3/4 cup	Water	1 cup plus 1 tablespoon
1 teaspoon	Grated lemon peel	1 1/2 teaspoons
1 tablespoon	Margarine or butter, softened	2 tablespoons
2 cups	Bread flour	3 cups
1 tablespoon	Dry milk	2 tablespoons
2 tablespoons	Sugar	3 tablespoons
1 teaspoon	Salt	1 1/2 teaspoons
1 1/4 teaspoons	Bread machine yeast	2 teaspoons
1/4 cup	Dried blueberries or currants	1/3 cup

Make 1 1/2-Pound Recipe with bread machines that use 3 cups flour, or make 1-Pound Recipe with bread machines that use 2 cups flour.

Measure carefully, placing all ingredients except blueberries in bread machine pan in the order recommended by the manufacturer. Add blueberries at the Raisin/Nut signal or 5 to 10 minutes before last kneading cycle ends.

Select Sweet or Basic/White cycle. Use Medium or Light crust color. Remove baked bread from pan and cool on wire rack.

Serving Size: 1 Slice Calories 160 (Calories from Fat 20); Fat 2g (Saturated 0g); Cholesterol 0mg; Sodium 290mg; Carbohydrate 33g; (Dietary Fiber 1g); Protein 4g

Gingered Pear Bread

1-Pound Recipe (8 slices)		1 1/2-Pound Recipe (12 slices)
2/3 cup	Water	1 cup plus 1 tablespoon
1 tablespoon	Margarine or butter, softened	2 tablespoons
2 cups	Bread flour	3 cups
1/4 cup	Cut-up dried pears	1/3 cup
2 teaspoons	Finely chopped crystallized ginger	1 tablespoon
1 tablespoon	Sugar	2 tablespoons
1 tablespoon	Dry milk	2 tablespoons
1 teaspoon	Salt	1 1/2 teaspoons
1 1/2 teaspoons	Bread machine yeast	2 teaspoons

Make 1 1/2-Pound Recipe with bread machines that use 3 cups flour, or make 1-Pound Recipe with bread machines that use 2 cups flour.

Measure carefully, placing all ingredients in bread machine pan in the order recommended by the manufacturer.

Select Sweet or Basic/White cycle. Use Medium or Light crust color. Remove baked bread from pan and cool on wire rack.

Serving Size: 1 Slice Calories 155 (Calories from Fat 20); Fat 2g (Saturated 0g); Cholesterol 0mg; Sodium 290mg; Carbohydrate 32g; (Dietary Fiber 2g); Protein 4g

Pineapple Aloha Bread

1-Pound Recipe (8 slices)		1 1/2-Pound Recipe (12 slices)
1/3 cup	Canned unsweetened crushed pineapple, drained*	3/4 cup
1/4 cup	Water	1/3 cup
2 tablespoons	Pineapple juice	1/4 cup
2 teaspoons	Margarine or butter, softened	1 tablespoon
2 cups	Bread flour	3 cups
1/3 cup	Toasted coconut	1/2 cup
1/4 cup	Pecan or walnut halves	1/3 cup
2 teaspoons	Dry milk	1 tablespoon
2 teaspoons	Brown sugar	1 tablespoon
3/4 teaspoon	Salt	1 teaspoon
1 teaspoon	Bread machine yeast	1 1/2 teaspoons

Make 1 1/2-Pound Recipe for bread machines that use 3 cups flour, or 1-Pound Recipe for bread machines that use 2 cups flour.

Measure all ingredients carefully and place in bread machine pan in the order recommended by the manufacturer.

Select Sweet or Basic/White cycle. Use Medium or Light crust color. Remove baked bread from pan and cool on wire rack.

*Save juice to use for the pineapple juice. If necessary, add water to pineapple juice to get required measurement.

Serving Size: 1 Slice Calories 170 (Calories from Fat 30); Fat 4g (Saturated 2g); Cholesterol 0mg; Sodium 200mg; Carbohydrate 33g; (Dietary Fiber 2g); Protein 4g

Panettone

1-Pound Recipe (8 slices)		1 1/2-Pound Recipe (12 slices)
2/3 cup	Water	3/4 cup plus 2 tablespoons
3 tablespoons	Margarine or butter, softened	1/4 cup (1/2 stick)
1	Egg	1
1 teaspoon	Vanilla	1 1/2 teaspoons
2 1/4 cups	Bread flour	3 1/4 cups
1 tablespoon	Sugar	2 tablespoons
1 tablespoon	Dry milk	2 tablespoons
1 teaspoon	Salt	1 1/2 teaspoons
1 1/4 teaspoons	Bread machine yeast	2 teaspoons
1/3 cup	Chopped mixed dried fruit	1/2 cup

Make 1 1/2-Pound Recipe with bread machines that use 3 cups flour, or make 1-Pound Recipe with bread machines that use 2 cups flour.

Measure carefully, placing all ingredients except fruit in bread machine pan in the order recommended by the manufacturer. Add fruit at the Raisin/Nut signal or 5 to 10 minutes before last kneading cycle ends.

Select Sweet or Basic/White cycle. Use Medium or Light crust color. Do not use delay cycles. Remove baked bread from pan and cool on wire rack.

Serving Size: 1 Slice Calories 195 (Calories from Fat 45); Fat 5g (Saturated 1g); Cholesterol 20mg; Sodium 320mg; Carbohydrate 35g; (Dietary Fiber 2g); Protein 5g

Sweet Lemon–Anise Loaf

1-Pound Recipe (8 slices)		1 1/2-Pound Recipe (12 slices)
3/4 cup	Water	1 cup plus 1 tablespoon
1 tablespoon	Margarine or butter, softened	2 tablespoons
2 cups	Bread flour	3 cups
1/4 cup	Sugar	1/3 cup
1 tablespoon	Dry milk	2 tablespoons
1 teaspoon	Anise seed, crushed	1 1/2 teaspoons
1 teaspoon	Grated lemon peel	1 1/2 teaspoons
3/4 teaspoon	Salt	1 teaspoon
1 1/2 teaspoons	Bread machine yeast	2 1/2 teaspoons

Make 1 1/2-Pound Recipe with bread machines that use 3 cups flour, or make 1-Pound Recipe with bread machines that use 2 cups flour.

Measure carefully, placing all ingredients in bread machine pan in the order recommended by the manufacturer.

Select Sweet or Basic/White cycle. Use Medium or Light crust color. Remove baked bread from pan and cool on wire rack. Serve with Lemon–Cream Cheese Spread (p. 86), if desired.

Serving Size: 1 Slice Calories 160 (Calories from Fat 20); Fat 2g (Saturated 0g); Cholesterol 0mg; Sodium 210mg; Carbohydrate 33g; (Dietary Fiber 1g); Protein 4g

Almond–Chocolate Chip Bread

1-Pound Recipe (8 slices)		1 1/2-Pound Recipe (12 slices)
3/4 cup plus 1 tablespoon	Water	1 cup plus 2 tablespoons
1 tablespoon	Margarine or butter, softened	2 tablespoons
1/4 teaspoon	Vanilla	1/2 teaspoon
2 cups	Bread flour	3 cups
1/2 cup	Semisweet chocolate chips	3/4 cup
2 tablespoons	Sugar	3 tablespoons
2 teaspoons	Dry milk	1 tablespoon
1/2 teaspoon	Salt	3/4 teaspoon
1 teaspoon	Bread machine yeast	1 1/2 teaspoons
1/4 cup	Sliced almonds	1/3 cup

Make 1 1/2-Pound Recipe with bread machines that use 3 cups flour, or make 1-Pound Recipe with bread machines that use 2 cups flour.

Measure carefully, placing all ingredients except almonds in bread machine pan in the order recommended by the manufacturer. Add almonds at the Raisin/Nut signal or 5 to 10 minutes before last kneading cycle ends.

Select Sweet or Basic/White cycle. Use Medium or Light crust color. Do not use delay cycles. Remove baked bread from pan and cool on wire rack.

Serving Size: 1 Slice Calories 225 (Calories from Fat 65); Fat 7g (Saturated 3g); Cholesterol 0mg; Sodium 160mg; Carbohydrate 37g; (Dietary Fiber 2g); Protein 5g

Cherry-Almond Loaf

1-Pound Recipe (8 slices)		1 1/2-Pound Recipe (12 slices)
2/3 cup	Water	3/4 cup plus 2 tablespoons
1/3 cup	Whole maraschino cherries, well-drained	1/2 cup
1 tablespoon	Margarine or butter, softened	2 tablespoons
2 cups	Bread flour	3 cups
1 tablespoon	Sugar	2 tablespoons
2 teaspoons	Dry milk	1 tablespoon
1 teaspoon	Salt	1 1/2 teaspoons
1 1/4 teaspoons	Bread machine yeast	2 teaspoons
1/4 cup	Slivered almonds	1/2 cup

Make 1 1/2-Pound Recipe with bread machines that use 3 cups flour, or make 1-Pound Recipe with bread machines that use 2 cups flour.

Measure carefully, placing all ingredients except almonds in bread machine pan in the order recommended by the manufacturer. Add almonds at the Raisin/Nut signal or 5 to 10 minutes before last kneading cycle ends.

Select Sweet or Basic/White cycle. Use Medium or Light crust color. Do not use delay cycles. Remove baked bread from pan and cool on wire rack.

Serving Size: 1 Slice Calories 185 (Calories from Fat 45); Fat 5g (Saturated 1g); Cholesterol 0mg; Sodium 290mg; Carbohydrate 32g; (Dietary Fiber 2g); Protein 5g

Almond–Chocolate Chip Bread

Coffee-Amaretto Bread

1-Pound Recipe (8 slices)		1 1/2-Pound Recipe (12 slices)
2 teaspoons	Instant coffee granules	1 tablespoon
3 tablespoons	Amaretto or other almond-flavored liqueur*	1/4 cup
1/2 cup plus 2 tablespoons	Water	3/4 cup plus 2 tablespoons
1 tablespoon	Margarine or butter, softened	2 tablespoons
2 cups	Bread flour	3 cups
3 tablespoons	Sugar	1/4 cup
1 tablespoon	Dry milk	2 tablespoons
3/4 teaspoon	Salt	1 1/4 teaspoons
1 1/2 teaspoons	Bread machine yeast	2 1/2 teaspoons

Make 1 1/2-Pound Recipe with bread machines that use 3 cups flour, or make 1-Pound Recipe with bread machines that use 2 cups flour.

Dissolve coffee granules in amaretto.

Measure carefully, placing coffee-amaretto mixture and remaining ingredients in bread machine pan in the order recommended by the manufacturer.

Select Sweet or Basic/White cycle. Use Medium or Light crust color. Remove baked bread from pan and cool on wire rack.

*Substitute 1 teaspoon almond extract plus enough water to equal 3 tablespoons for the 3 tablespoons amaretto or 2 teaspoons almond extract plus enough water to equal 1/4 cup for the 1/4 cup amaretto.

Serving Size: 1 Slice Calories 170 (Calories from Fat 20); Fat 2g (Saturated 1g); Cholesterol 0mg; Sodium 250mg; Carbohydrate 33g; (Dietary Fiber 1g); Protein 4g

Julekage

This is one of Scandinavia's most popular Christmas coffee cakes!

1 Pound Recipe (8 slices)		1 1/2-Pound Recipe (12 slices)
1 egg plus enough water to measure 3/4 cup	Egg	1 egg plus enough water to measure 1 cup plus 2 tablespoons
1/4 teaspoon	Ground cardamom	1/2 teaspoon
3/4 teaspoon	Salt	1 teaspoon
2 teaspoons	Sugar	1 tablespoon plus 1 teaspoon
1/4 cup (1/2 stick)	Butter, softened*	1/4 cup (1/2 stick) plus 2 tablespoons
2 cups	Bread flour	3 cups
1/2 teaspoon	Bread machine yeast	1 teaspoon
1/4 cup	Raisins	1/3 cup
1/4 cup	Fruit cake mix (mixed candied fruit)	1/3 cup

Make 1 1/2-Pound Recipe with bread machines that use 3 cups flour, or make 1-Pound Recipe with bread machines that use 2 cups flour.

Measure carefully, placing all ingredients except raisins and fruit in bread machine pan in the order recommended by the manufacturer. Add raisins and fruit at the Raisin/Nut signal or 5 to 10 minutes before last kneading cycle ends.

Select Sweet or Basic/White cycle. Use Medium or Light crust color. Do not use delay cycles. Remove baked bread from pan and cool on wire rack.

*We do not recommend margarine for this recipe.

Serving Size: 1 Slice Calories 215 (Calories from Fat 65); Fat 7g (Saturated 4g); Cholesterol 35mg; Sodium 240mg; Carbohydrate 35g; (Dietary Fiber 1g); Protein 4g

French Baguettes, Sun-dried Tomato Olive Oil (p. 82)

Breads in All Shapes—
Savory and Sweet

French Baguettes

2 loaves, 12 slices each

This versatile bread is great eaten fresh from the oven, or you can use it to make everything from sub sandwiches to garlic bread.

1 cup water
2 1/2 cups bread flour
1 tablespoon sugar
1 teaspoon salt
1 1/2 teaspoons bread machine yeast
1 egg yolk
1 tablespoon water

Measure carefully, placing all ingredients except egg yolk and 1 tablespoon water in bread machine pan in the order recommended by the manufacturer.

Select Dough/Manual cycle.

Place dough in greased bowl, turning to coat all sides. Cover and let rise in warm place about 30 minutes or until double. (Dough is ready if indentation remains when touched.)

Grease cookie sheet. Punch down dough. Roll dough into rectangle, 16×12 inches, on lightly floured surface. Cut dough crosswise in half. Roll up each half of dough tightly, beginning at 12-inch side. Roll gently back and forth to taper ends.

Place 3 inches apart on cookie sheet. Make 1/4-inch-deep diagonal slashes across loaves every 2 inches, or make 1 lengthwise slash on each loaf. Cover and let rise in warm place 30 to 40 minutes or until double.

Heat oven to 375°. Mix egg yolk and 1 tablespoon water; brush over tops of loaves. Bake 20 to 25 minutes or until golden brown. Serve warm, or cool on wire rack. Serve with Sundried Tomato Olive Oil (p. 82), if desired. To serve, place oil in shallow bowl or small plate with rim; dip bread into oil.

Serving Size: 1 Slice Calories 50 (Calories from Fat 0); Fat 0g (Saturated 0g); Cholesterol 10mg; Sodium 90mg; Carbohydrate 12g; (Dietary Fiber 0g); Protein 1g

French Onion Tart

10 pieces

3/4 cup water
1 tablespoon margarine or butter, softened
2 cups bread flour
2 tablespoons dry milk
1 tablespoon sugar
1 teaspoon salt
1 1/4 teaspoons bread machine yeast
Onion Topping (below)
2 cans (2 ounces each) anchovy fillets, drained
10 oil-cured Greek olives, cut in half and pitted

Measure carefully, placing all ingredients except Onion Topping, anchovy fillets and olives in bread machine pan in the order recommended by the manufacturer.

Select Dough/Manual Cycle.

Grease cookie sheet lightly. Prepare Onion Topping.

Shape dough into flattened rectangle on floured surface. Let dough rest 15 minutes. Roll dough with floured rolling pin into rectangle, 14×11 inches. Place on cookie sheet. (Reshape dough if necessary after moving to cookie sheet.)

Spoon Onion Topping evenly over dough to within 1 inch of edge. Arrange anchovy fillets in lattice pattern on topping. Top with olives. Let tart rest 15 minutes.

Heat oven to 425°. Bake 15 to 20 minutes or until crust is brown. Serve warm.

ONION TOPPING

3 tablespoons olive or vegetable oil
3 large onions, thinly sliced
1 tablespoon chopped fresh or 1 teaspoon dried basil leaves
1/4 teaspoon white pepper

Heat oil in 10-inch skillet over medium heat. Stir in onions; reduce heat. Cover and cook 25 minutes, stirring occasionally, until onions are tender. Stir in basil and white pepper.

Serving Size: 1 Piece Calories 185 (Calories from Fat 65); Fat 7g (Saturated 1g); Cholesterol 10mg; Sodium 600mg; Carbohydrate 27g; (Dietary Fiber 2g); Protein 6g

French Onion Tart

Challah Braid

12 slices

Loaves of this bread make a perfect housewarming present! For an extra special gift, present it on a shiny new cookie sheet.

   3/4 cup plus 1 tablespoon water
   1 egg
   2 tablespoons margarine or butter, softened
   3 1/4 cups bread flour
   2 tablespoons sugar
   1 1/2 teaspoons salt
   1 1/2 teaspoons bread machine yeast
   1 egg yolk
   2 tablespoons cold water
   1 tablespoon poppy seed

Measure carefully, placing all ingredients except egg yolk, cold water and poppy seed in bread machine pan in the order recommended by the manufacturer.

Select Dough/Manual cycle.

Grease large cookie sheet. Place dough on lightly floured surface. Divide dough into 3 equal pieces. Roll each piece into 13-inch rope. Place ropes close together on cookie sheet. Braid gently and loosely (do not stretch). Pinch ends to seal; tuck ends under braid. Cover and let rise in warm place about 45 minutes or until double.

Heat oven to 375°. Mix egg yolk and cold water; brush over braid. Sprinkle with poppy seed. Bake about 25 minutes or until golden brown. Serve with Lemon–Poppy Seed Butter (p. 81), if desired.

Serving Size: 1 Slice Calories 165 (Calories from Fat 25); Fat 3g (Saturated 1g); Cholesterol 35mg; Sodium 300mg; Carbohydrate 31g; (Dietary Fiber 1g); Protein 5g

Caramelized Onion Focaccia

8 pieces

   3/4 cup water
   2 tablespoons olive or vegetable oil
   2 cups bread flour
   1 tablespoon sugar
   1 teaspoon salt
   1 1/2 teaspoons bread machine yeast
   Onion Topping (below)
   3/4 cup shredded mozzarella cheese (3 ounces)
   2 tablespoons grated Parmesan cheese

Measure carefully, placing all ingredients except Onion Topping and cheeses in bread machine pan in the order recommended by the manufacturer.

Select Dough/Manual cycle.

Grease cookie sheet. Pat dough into 12-inch circle on cookie sheet. Cover and let rise in warm place about 30 minutes or until almost double. Prepare Onion Topping.

Heat oven to 400°. Make deep depressions in dough at 1-inch intervals with finger or handle of wooden spoon. Spread topping over dough. Sprinkle with cheeses. Bake 15 to 18 minutes or until edge is golden brown. Remove from cookie sheet to wire rack. Cut into wedges; serve warm.

Onion Topping

   3 tablespoons margarine or butter
   2 medium onions, sliced
   2 cloves garlic, finely chopped

Melt margarine in 10-inch skillet over medium-low heat. Cook onions and garlic in margarine 15 to 20 minutes, stirring occasionally, until onions are brown and caramelized; remove from heat.

Serving Size: 1 Piece Calories 235 (Calories from Fat 90); Fat 10g (Saturated 3g); Cholesterol 5mg; Sodium 400mg; Carbohydrate 31g; (Dietary Fiber 2g); Protein 7g

Caramelized Onion Focaccia

Cheesy Garlic Monkey Bread

10 slices

3/4 cup water
1 egg
1/4 cup shortening
3 1/2 cups bread flour
1/3 cup sugar
1 teaspoon salt
1 1/2 teaspoons bread machine yeast
1/3 cup grated Parmesan cheese
4 cloves garlic, finely chopped
1/2 cup (1 stick) margarine or butter, melted

Measure carefully, placing all ingredients except cheese, garlic and margarine in bread machine pan in the order recommended by the manufacturer.

Select Dough/Manual cycle.

Grease tube pan, 10×4 inches, or 12-cup bundt cake pan. Divide dough into 20 equal pieces. Mix cheese and garlic. Dip dough pieces into melted margarine, then roll in cheese mixture. Arrange in layers in pan. Cover and let rise in warm place about 45 minutes or until double.

Heat oven to 350°. Bake 35 to 45 minutes or until golden brown. Remove from pan. Serve warm.

Serving Size: 1 Slice Calories 340 (Calories from Fat 145); Fat 16g (Saturated 4g); Cholesterol 25mg; Sodium 380mg; Carbohydrate 44g; (Dietary Fiber 2g); Protein 7g

Favorite Cheese Pizza

2 pizzas, 6 pieces each

In addition to the Pizza Topping, you have creative license to add your own favorite toppings to make your own masterpiece.

1 cup plus 2 tablespoons water
2 tablespoons olive or vegetable oil
3 cups bread flour
2 tablespoons grated Parmesan cheese, if desired
1 1/2 teaspoons Italian seasoning, if desired
1 teaspoon sugar
1 teaspoon salt
2 1/2 teaspoons bread machine yeast
Pizza Topping (below)

Measure carefully, placing all ingredients except Pizza Topping in bread machine pan in the order recommended by the manufacturer.

Select Dough/Manual cycle.

Move oven rack to lowest position. Heat oven to 400°.

Grease 2 cookie sheets. Divide dough in half. Pat each half into 12-inch circle on cookie sheet with floured fingers. Add Pizza Topping.

Bake 18 to 20 minutes or until crust is light brown.

Pizza Topping

1 can (8 ounces) tomato sauce
1 teaspoon Italian seasoning
1 clove garlic, finely chopped
1 small onion, thinly sliced and separated into rings
3 cups shredded mozzarella cheese (12 ounces)
1/4 cup grated Parmesan cheese

Mix tomato sauce, Italian seasoning and garlic. Spread half the sauce over each crust. Arrange onion on sauce. Sprinkle with cheeses.

Serving Size: 1 Piece Calories 230 (Calories from Fat 70); Fat 8g (Saturated 4g); Cholesterol 15mg; Sodium 470mg; Carbohydrate 30g; (Dietary Fiber 2g); Protein 12g

Favorite Cheese Pizza

Rosemary Focaccia

8 pieces

Focaccia is a popular Italian flatbread.

3/4 cup water
2 tablespoons olive or vegetable oil
2 cups bread flour
1 tablespoon sugar
1 teaspoon salt
1 1/2 teaspoons bread machine yeast
3 tablespoons olive or vegetable oil
2 to 3 tablespoons chopped fresh rosemary
Fresh coarsely ground pepper, if desired

Measure carefully, placing all ingredients except 3 tablespoons oil, the rosemary and pepper in bread machine pan in the order recommended by the manufacturer.

Select Dough/Manual cycle.

Grease cookie sheet. Pat dough into 12-inch circle on cookie sheet. Cover and let rise in warm place about 30 minutes or until almost double.

Heat oven to 400°. Make deep depressions in dough at 1-inch intervals with finger or handle of wooden spoon. Drizzle with 3 tablespoons oil. Sprinkle with rosemary and pepper.

Bake 15 to 18 minutes or until edge is golden brown. Remove from cookie sheet to wire rack. Cut into wedges; serve warm.

Serving Size: 1 Piece Calories 205 (Calories from Fat 80); Fat 9g (Saturated 1g); Cholesterol 0mg; Sodium 270mg; Carbohydrate 28g; (Dietary Fiber 1g); Protein 4g

Shrimp and Scallop Pizza

6 pieces

1/2 cup plus 1 tablespoon water
1 tablespoon olive or vegetable oil
1 1/2 cups bread flour
1/2 teaspoon sugar
1/2 teaspoon salt
1 1/4 teaspoons bread machine yeast
2 tablespoons olive or vegetable oil
3 cloves garlic, finely chopped
Pizza Topping (below)

Measure carefully, placing all ingredients except 2 tablespoons oil, the garlic and Pizza Topping in bread machine pan in the order recommended by the manufacturer.

Select Dough/Manual cycle. Mix 2 tablespoons olive oil and the garlic; let stand at room temperature.

Grease 12-inch pizza pan with olive oil. Place dough in pizza pan; cover and let rest 15 minutes.

Move oven rack to lowest position. Heat oven to 500°. Press dough in bottom and up side of pan with lightly oiled fingers. Brush about half the garlic-oil mixture over dough. Add Pizza Topping. Drizzle remaining garlic-oil mixture over top of pizza.

Bake about 10 minutes or until seafood is done and cheeses are melted.

PIZZA TOPPING

1 cup shredded mozzarella cheese (8 ounces)
1/2 cup shredded provolone cheese (4 ounces)
18 uncooked shelled and deveined medium
  shrimp
1/2 pound bay scallops
1/4 cup chopped fresh basil leaves

Mix cheeses; sprinkle over dough. Place shrimp and scallops on cheeses. Sprinkle with basil.

Serving Size: 1 Piece Calories 420 (Calories from Fat 180); Fat 20g (Saturated 9g); Cholesterol 80mg; Sodium 700mg; Carbohydrate 30g; (Dietary Fiber 1g); Protein 31g

Family Pizza with Fresh Tomato Sauce

16 pieces

1 cup plus 2 tablespoons water
2 tablespoons olive or vegetable oil
3 cups bread flour
1 teaspoon sugar
1 teaspoon salt
2 1/2 teaspoons bread machine yeast
2 teaspoons olive or vegetable oil
2 cups shredded mozzarella cheese (8 ounces)
1 pound bulk Italian sausage or ground beef, cooked and drained
Fresh Tomato Sauce (below)
1/2 cup shredded Parmesan cheese

Measure carefully, placing water, 2 tablespoons oil, the flour, sugar, salt and yeast in bread machine pan in the order recommended by the manufacturer.

Select Dough/Manual cycle.

Grease jelly roll pan, 15 1/2×10 1/2×1 inch, with olive oil. Place dough in pan; cover and let rest 15 minutes.

Move oven rack to lowest position. Heat oven to 425°. Press dough in bottom and up sides of pan with lightly oiled fingers. Brush 2 teaspoons oil over dough. Sprinkle with 1 cup of the mozzarella cheese. Top with sausage, Fresh Tomato Sauce, remaining 1 cup mozzarella cheese and the Parmesan cheese.

Bake 25 to 30 minutes or until crust is brown and cheese is melted and bubbly. Let stand 10 minutes before cutting.

FRESH TOMATO SAUCE

3 cups chopped seeded tomatoes* (3 medium)
1 cup sliced mushrooms (3 ounces)
1/2 cup chopped onion (1 medium)
1/4 cup chopped fresh parsley
1 tablespoon chopped fresh or 1 teaspoon dried basil leaves
1 tablespoon chopped fresh or 1 teaspoon dried oregano leaves
1 teaspoon salt
2 cloves garlic, finely chopped

Mix all ingredients.

*We do not recommend hydroponic tomatoes for this recipe because of their high moisture content.

Serving Size: 1 Piece Calories 260 (Calories from Fat 115); Fat 13g (Saturated 5g); Cholesterol 30mg; Sodium 650mg; Carbohydrate 23g; (Dietary Fiber 1g); Protein 14g

Easy Family Pizza: Substitute 3 1/2 cups prepared thick, chunky spaghetti sauce with mushrooms for the Fresh Tomato Sauce.

Deep-Dish Pizza with Fresh Tomato Sauce: Grease 2 round pans, 9×1 1/2 inches, with olive oil. Divide dough in half. Place dough in pans; cover and let rest 15 minutes. Press dough in bottom and up sides of pans with lightly oiled fingers. Brush half of the 2 teaspoons oil over dough in each pan. Sprinkle each with 1/2 cup of the mozzarella cheese. Top each with half the sausage, Fresh Tomato Sauce, remaining 1 cup mozzarella cheese and the Parmesan cheese. Bake 25 to 30 minutes or until crust is brown and cheese is melted and bubbly. Let stand 10 minutes before cutting.

Italian Salami Sandwich Loaf

8 pieces

3/4 cup water
1 tablespoon margarine or butter, softened
2 cups bread flour
2 tablespoons dry milk
1 tablespoon sugar
1 teaspoon salt
1 1/4 teaspoons bread machine yeast
2 cups chopped green bell peppers (2 medium)
1/2 cup chopped onion (1 medium)
1 cup chopped salami (1/4 pound)
1/4 cup shredded mozzarella cheese (1 ounce)
1/4 cup grated Parmesan cheese

Measure carefully, placing water, margarine, flour, dry milk, sugar, salt and yeast in bread machine pan in the order recommended by the manufacturer.

Select Dough/Manual cycle.

Divide dough into 3 equal pieces; cover and let rest 15 minutes.

Move oven rack to lowest position. Heat oven to 375°. Grease cookie sheet. Roll one piece of dough into 7-inch circle on lightly floured surface. (Let dough rest 5 minutes longer if difficult to roll.) Place on cookie sheet. Sprinkle with half the bell peppers, onion, salami and cheeses to within 1 inch of edge.

Roll second piece of dough into 7-inch circle; place over cheeses. Sprinkle with remaining ingredients. Roll remaining piece of dough into 8-inch circle; place on top. Carefully fold edge of top dough circle under bottom dough circle, stretching dough slightly if necessary; seal securely.

Bake about 45 minutes or until deep golden brown. Cut into wedges; serve warm.

Serving Size: **1 Piece** Calories 230 (Calories from Fat 70); Fat 8g (Saturated 3g); Cholesterol 15mg; Sodium 620mg; Carbohydrate 31g; (Dietary Fiber 2g); Protein 10g

---

Bread Baking Tips

Sometimes when we make new bread recipes, we come across little problems along the way. Here are some troubleshooting tips to help the bread you make turn out perfect every time.

WHAT DO YOU DO IF:

You can't shape the dough when the bread machine cycle is completed? Just punch it down to get out the air, cover and let rise again. (The next rising may take a bit less time.)

The dough springs back when rolling out? When dough springs back again and again as you roll it, just cover it with a towel and allow it to rest 5 to 10 minutes. Dough will relax and roll out more easily.

Shaped dough rises too high? Dough has risen too long or at too high a temperature. Never set dough to rise in a heated oven or in direct sunlight. A temperature of 80° to 85° is just right. If the shaped dough doesn't have a filling, turn it onto a flat surface, press or roll out the air bubbles, reshape and let rise again before baking.

Bread has big air holes after baking? Next time, firmly punch down dough before shaping and press and roll out gas bubbles.

Italian Salami Sandwich Loaf

Savory Calzones

6 calzones

1 cup water
1 tablespoon olive or vegetable oil
2 1/2 cups bread flour
1 teaspoon sugar
1 teaspoon salt
2 1/4 teaspoons bread machine yeast
Savory Filling (below)
1 egg, slightly beaten

Measure carefully, placing all ingredients except Savory Filling and egg in bread machine pan in the order recommended by the manufacturer.

Select Dough/Manual cycle.

Heat oven to 375°. Grease cookie sheet. Divide dough into 6 equal pieces. Roll each piece into 7-inch circle on lightly floured surface with floured rolling pin. Add Savory Filling.

Fold dough over filling; fold edge up and pinch securely to seal. Place on cookie sheet. Brush with egg. Bake 25 to 30 minutes or until golden brown.

SAVORY FILLING

6 sun-dried tomato halves (not oil-packed)
1/3 cup pesto
1 1/2 cups shredded mozzarella or provolone cheese (6 ounces)
4 ounces Canadian-style bacon or ham, cut into thin strips (about 1 cup)
1 cup sliced mushrooms (3 ounces)
Freshly ground pepper

Soak tomatoes in 1 cup very hot water about 10 minutes or until softened; drain and finely chop. Spread 1 tablespoon pesto on each circle to within 1 inch of edge. Layer cheese, bacon, mushrooms and tomatoes on half of each circle to within 1 inch of edge. Sprinkle with pepper.

Serving Size: 1 Calzone Calories 450 (Calories from Fat 180); Fat 20g (Saturated 6g); Cholesterol 60mg; Sodium 850mg; Carbohydrate 49g; (Dietary Fiber 3g); Protein 21g

Miniature Brioche

12 brioche

1/4 cup water
3 tablespoons margarine or butter, softened
2 eggs
2 1/2 cups bread flour
1/4 cup sugar
3/4 teaspoon salt
1 teaspoon grated orange or lemon peel
2 1/2 teaspoons bread machine yeast
1 tablespoon milk
1 egg yolk
Coarse sugar crystals

Measure carefully, placing all ingredients except milk, egg yolk and sugar crystals in bread machine pan in the order recommended by the manufacturer.

Select Dough/Manual cycle.

Place dough in greased bowl, turning to coat all sides. Cover with plastic wrap and refrigerate at least 4 hours, but no longer than 24 hours.

Grease 12 medium muffin cups, 2 1/2×1 1/4 inches. Punch down dough. Divide dough into 16 equal pieces; roll into balls. Cut 4 balls into 3 pieces each; roll into small balls. Place 12 large balls in muffin cups. Flatten and make an indentation in center of each with thumb. Place 1 small ball in each indentation. Cover and let rise in warm place 50 to 60 minutes or until double.

Heat oven to 350°. Mix milk and egg yolk; gently brush over tops of rolls. Sprinkle with sugar crystals. Bake 15 to 20 minutes or until golden brown. Remove from pan. Serve warm.

Serving Size: 1 Brioche Calories 165 (Calories from Fat 35); Fat 4g (Saturated 1g); Cholesterol 55mg; Sodium 180mg; Carbohydrate 29g; (Dietary Fiber 1g); Protein 4g

Whole Wheat Dinner Rolls

12 rolls

Bring back memories of grandmother's kitchen and treat your family to the heavenly aroma of homemade rolls baking in the oven.

3/4 cup water
1 tablespoon shortening
1 1/4 cups bread flour
1 cup whole wheat flour
2 tablespoons packed brown sugar
1 tablespoon dry milk
1/2 teaspoon salt
1 1/4 teaspoons bread machine yeast

Measure carefully, placing all ingredients in bread machine pan in the order recommended by the manufacturer.

Select Dough/Manual cycle.

Grease large cookie sheet. Punch down dough; place on lightly floured surface. Divide dough into 12 equal pieces. Shape each piece into a ball. Place slightly apart on cookie sheet. Cover and let rise in warm place about 30 minutes or until double.

Heat oven to 375°. Bake 15 to 20 minutes or until golden brown.

Serving Size: **1 Roll** Calories 100 (Calories from Fat 10); Fat 1g (Saturated 0g); Cholesterol 0mg; Sodium 90mg; Carbohydrate 21g; (Dietary Fiber 1g); Protein 3g

Savory Breadsticks

30 breadsticks

Just for fun, try twisting each 8-inch strip into a pretzel shape before baking.

1 cup plus 2 tablespoons water
3 tablespoons margarine or butter, softened
3 cups bread flour
2 tablespoons sugar
1 1/2 teaspoons salt
2 teaspoons dried rosemary leaves, crushed
1 teaspoon dried oregano leaves, crushed
2 1/4 teaspoons bread machine yeast
1 tablespoon water
1 egg white

Measure carefully, placing all ingredients except 1 tablespoon water and the egg white in bread machine pan in the order recommended by the manufacturer.

Select Dough/Manual cycle.

Grease cookie sheet. Divide dough into 30 equal pieces. Roll each piece into 8-inch rope. Place 1 inch apart on cookie sheet. Cover and let rise in warm place 20 to 25 minutes or until puffy.

Heat oven to 350°. Beat 1 tablespoon water and the egg white; brush over dough. Bake 15 to 20 minutes or until golden brown.

Serving Size: **1 Breadstick** Calories 55 (Calories from Fat 10); Fat 1g (Saturated 0g); Cholesterol 0mg; Sodium 120mg; Carbohydrate 11g; (Dietary Fiber 0g); Protein 1g

French Twists

18 twists

3/4 cup water
2 cups bread flour
1 tablespoon sugar
1 teaspoon salt
1 1/2 teaspoons bread machine yeast
1/3 cup margarine or butter, melted
1 egg yolk
1 tablespoon water

Measure first 5 ingredients carefully and place in bread machine pan in the order recommended by the manufacturer.

Select Dough/Manual cycle. Grease 2 cookie sheets.

Divide dough into 18 equal pieces. Roll each piece into 14- to 16-inch rope on lightly floured surface. Bring ends together; twist 3 or 4 times. Place on cookie sheets. Brush generously with melted margarine. Cover and let rise in warm place 20 to 30 minutes or until double.

Heat oven to 400°. Mix egg yolk and 1 tablespoon water; brush over twists. Bake 12 to 15 minutes or until golden brown.

Serving Size: 1 Twist Calories 90 (Calories from Fat 35); Fat 4g (Saturated 1g); Cholesterol 10mg; Sodium 160mg; Carbohydrate 12g; (Dietary Fiber 0g); Protein 2g

Wild Rice Breadsticks

10 breadsticks

The wild rice in these breadsticks gives them a great, nutty flavor.

3/4 cup water
1 tablespoon vegetable oil
1 tablespoon molasses
1 2/3 cups bread flour
1/2 cup whole wheat flour
1/2 cup cooked wild rice or brown rice
1 teaspoon fennel seed, if desired
1 teaspoon salt
1 teaspoon bread machine yeast

Measure carefully, placing all ingredients in bread machine pan in the order recommended by the manufacturer.

Select Dough/Manual cycle.

Grease large cookie sheet. Divide dough into 10 equal pieces. Roll each piece into 9-inch rope. Place on cookie sheet. Brush with vegetable oil. Cover and let rise in warm place 5 to 15 minutes or until slightly risen.

Heat oven to 375°. To make breadsticks resemble sheaves of grain, make short angled cuts with scissors at one end of each breadstick. For a shiny finish, brush breadsticks with slightly beaten egg, if desired. Bake 15 to 20 minutes or until golden brown. Remove from cookie sheet to wire rack. Serve warm or cool.

Serving Size: 1 Breadstick Calories 125 (Calories from Fat 20); Fat 2g (Saturated 0g); Cholesterol 0mg; Sodium 220mg; Carbohydrate 25g; (Dietary Fiber 1g); Protein 3g

Wild Rice Breadsticks, Double Apricot–Almond Bread (p. 49), Fireside Cheddar-Olive Bread (p. 27)

Coconut-Pecan Braid

16 slices

3/4 cup plus 1 tablespoon water
1 tablespoon margarine or butter, softened
2 cups bread flour
2 tablespoons dry milk
1 tablespoon sugar
1 teaspoon salt
1 teaspoon bread machine yeast
Coconut-Pecan Filling (below)
1/4 cup (1/2 stick) margarine or butter, softened
Powdered sugar

Measure carefully, placing all ingredients except Coconut-Pecan Filling, 1/4 cup margarine and the powdered sugar in bread machine pan in the order recommended by the manufacturer.

Select Dough/Manual cycle.

Grease jelly roll pan, 15 1/2×10 1/2×1 inch. Place dough on lightly floured surface; cover and let rest 15 minutes.

Prepare Coconut-Pecan Filling. Roll dough into rectangle, 15×10 inches. (Let dough rest 5 minutes longer if difficult to roll.) Spread with 1/4 cup margarine. Sprinkle with filling; press into dough.

Roll up rectangle, beginning at 15-inch side. Cut roll lengthwise in half. Place strips, filling sides up, side-by-side in pan. Twist together gently and loosely. Cover and let rise about 45 minutes or until double.

Heat oven to 350°. Bake 25 to 30 minutes until golden brown. Immediately remove from pan; cool slightly. Sprinkle with powdered sugar.

COCONUT-PECAN FILLING

1/2 cup flaked coconut
1/2 cup chopped pecans
1/2 cup packed brown sugar
2 tablespoons milk
2 tablespoons margarine or butter, melted
1 teaspoon ground cinnamon

Mix all ingredients.

Serving Size: 1 Slice Calories 180 (Calories from Fat 80); Fat 9g (Saturated 2g); Cholesterol 0mg; Sodium 200mg; Carbohydrate 24g; (Dietary Fiber 1g); Protein 2g

Caramel-Pecan Rolls

9 rolls

3/4 cup plus 2 tablespoons water
2 tablespoons margarine or butter, softened
2 1/2 cups bread flour
1/4 cup sugar
1 teaspoon salt
1 teaspoon bread machine yeast
Caramel Topping (below)
Cinnamon Filling (below)
2 tablespoons margarine or butter, softened

Measure carefully, placing all ingredients except Caramel Topping, Cinnamon Filling and 2 tablespoons margarine in bread machine pan in the order recommended by the manufacturer.

Select Dough/Manual cycle.

Prepare Caramel Topping and Cinnamon Filling.

Flatten dough with hands or rolling pin into 9-inch square on lightly floured surface. Spread with 2 tablespoons margarine; sprinkle with Cinnamon Filling. Roll dough up tightly; pinch edge of dough into roll to seal. Cut roll into 1-inch slices. Place in pan. Cover and let rise in warm place about 1 hour or until double.

Heat oven to 375°. Bake 22 to 27 minutes or until golden brown. Immediately invert pan onto heatproof serving plate or tray. Let stand 1 minute so caramel can drizzle over rolls. Serve warm.

CARAMEL TOPPING

1/4 cup (1/2 stick) margarine or butter, melted
1/3 cup packed brown sugar
1 tablespoon corn syrup
1/2 cup pecan halves

Place margarine in ungreased square pan, 9×9×2 inches. Stir in brown sugar and corn syrup until well blended. Spread evenly in pan. Sprinkle with pecans.

CINNAMON FILLING

1/3 cup granulated sugar
1 1/2 teaspoons ground cinnamon

Mix ingredients.

Serving Size: 1 Roll Calories 360 (Calories from Fat 135); Fat 15g (Saturated 3g); Cholesterol 0mg; Sodium 360mg; Carbohydrate 53g; (Dietary Fiber 2g); Protein 5g

Cardamom Twists

12 twists

3/4 cup milk
2 tablespoons margarine or butter, softened
2 cups bread flour
1/4 cup sugar
3/4 teaspoon salt
1/2 teaspoon ground cardamom
2 teaspoons bread machine yeast
1 egg, beaten

Measure carefully, placing all ingredients except egg in bread machine pan in the order recommended by the manufacturer.

Select Dough/Manual cycle.

Grease large cookie sheet. Divide dough into 12 equal pieces. Roll each piece into 12-inch rope (lightly flour surface, if necessary). Bring ends of each rope together; twist 2 or 3 times. Place 2 inches apart on cookie sheet. Cover and let rise in warm place 30 to 40 minutes or until almost double.

Heat oven to 375°. Brush dough lightly with egg. Bake 10 to 14 minutes or until golden brown. Serve warm, or cool on wire rack.

Serving Size: 1 Twist Calories 125 (Calories from Fat 25); Fat 3g (Saturated 1g); Cholesterol 20mg; Sodium 170mg; Carbohydrate 23g; (Dietary Fiber 1g); Protein 3g

Parmesan-Garlic Twists

18 twists

These simple breadsticks get rave reviews. Since they pack and travel well, they are the perfect bring-along bread whether you're going on a picnic or to someone's house for dinner.

3/4 cup water
2 cups bread flour
1 tablespoon sugar
1 teaspoon salt
1 1/2 teaspoons bread machine yeast
1/3 cup margarine or butter, melted
2 tablespoons grated Parmesan cheese
2 cloves garlic, finely chopped

Measure carefully, placing all ingredients except margarine, cheese and garlic in bread machine pan in the order recommended by the manufacturer.

Select Dough/Manual cycle. Grease 2 cookie sheets.

Divide dough into 18 equal pieces. Roll each piece into 14- to 16-inch rope on lightly floured surface. Bring ends together; twist 3 or 4 times. Place on cookie sheets.

Mix margarine, garlic and cheese. Brush twists generously with cheese mixture. Cover and let rise in warm place 20 to 30 minutes or until double.

Heat oven to 400°. Bake 12 to 15 minutes or until golden brown.

Serving Size: 1 Twist Calories 95 (Calories from Fat 35); Fat 4g (Saturated 1g); Cholesterol 0mg; Sodium 170mg; Carbohydrate 13g; (Dietary Fiber 0g); Protein 2g

Fruited Coffee Cake

Fruited Coffee Cake

16 pieces

This festive fruit-filled coffee cake is perfect wrapped for any gift-giving occasion.

3/4 cup water
2 tablespoons margarine or butter, softened
1 cup bread flour
1 cup whole wheat flour
2 tablespoons packed brown sugar
1 teaspoon salt
1 1/2 teaspoons bread machine yeast
1 cup canned fruit pie filling (apple, apricot, blueberry, cherry)
Powdered sugar or Vanilla Glaze (p. 79), if desired.

Measure carefully, placing all ingredients except pie filling in bread machine pan in the order recommended by the manufacturer.

Select Dough/Manual cycle.

Grease cookie sheet. Roll dough into 13×8-inch rectangle on lightly floured surface; place on cookie sheet. Spread pie filling lengthwise down center third of rectangle. Make cuts 2 inches long at 1-inch intervals on each 13-inch side of rectangle. Fold strips at an angle over filling, overlapping and crossing in center. Cover and let rise in warm place 30 to 45 minutes or until double.

Heat oven to 375°. Bake 30 to 35 minutes or until golden brown. Remove from cookie sheet to wire rack; cool. Sprinkle with powdered sugar or drizzle with Vanilla Glaze.

Serving Size: 1 Piece Calories 100 (Calories from Fat 20); Fat 2g (Saturated 0g); Cholesterol 0mg; Sodium 150mg; Carbohydrate 19g; (Dietary Fiber 1g); Protein 2g

Sticky Orange Rolls

12 rolls

1 cup water
1/4 cup (1/2 stick) margarine or butter, softened
3 1/2 cups bread flour
1/3 cup packed brown sugar
1 teaspoon salt
1 1/2 teaspoons bread machine yeast
1/2 cup (1 stick) margarine or butter, melted
2 tablespoons grated orange peel
1/2 cup granulated sugar

Measure carefully, placing all ingredients except 1/2 cup melted margarine, the orange peel and granulated sugar in bread machine pan in the order recommended by the manufacturer.

Select Dough/Manual cycle.

Grease rectangular pan, 13×9×2 inches. Divide dough in half. Roll each half into 12-inch rope on lightly floured surface. Cut each rope into 6 pieces.

Mix 1/2 cup melted margarine, the orange peel and granulated sugar in medium bowl. Dip dough pieces into orange mixture, covering dough completely. Place slightly apart in pan. Cover and let rise in warm place about 30 minutes or until double.

Heat oven to 350°. Bake 20 to 30 minutes or until golden brown.

Sticky Orange-Almond Rolls: Place 1 cup sliced unblanched almonds in small bowl. Roll dough pieces in almonds after dipping into orange mixture.

Note: If you prefer evenly shaped rolls, roll dough pieces into balls before dipping into orange mixture.

Serving Size: 1 Roll Calories 305 (Calories from Fat 110); Fat 12g (Saturated 3g); Cholesterol 0mg; Sodium 310mg; Carbohydrate 45g; (Dietary Fiber 1g); Protein 4g

Glazed Cinnamon Rolls

Glazed Cinnamon Rolls

9 rolls

These cinnamon rolls are easy to whip together, perfect for any breakfast or brunch.

    3/4 cup plus 2 tablespoons water
    2 tablespoons margarine or butter, softened
    2 1/2 cups bread flour
    1/4 cup sugar
    1 teaspoon salt
    1 teaspoons bread machine yeast
    Cinnamon Filling (below)
    2 tablespoons margarine or butter, softened
    Vanilla Glaze (below)

Measure carefully, placing all ingredients except Cinnamon Filling, 2 tablespoons margarine and Vanilla Glaze in bread machine pan in the order recommended by the manufacturer.

Select Dough/Manual cycle.

Grease square pan, 9×9×2 inches. Prepare Cinnamon Filling.

Flatten dough with hands or rolling pin into 9-inch square on lightly floured surface. Spread with 2 tablespoons margarine; sprinkle with Cinnamon Filling. Roll dough up tightly; pinch edge of dough into roll to seal. Cut roll into 1-inch slices. Place in pan. Cover and let rise in warm place 1 to 1 1/4 hours or until double.

Heat oven to 375°. Bake 25 to 30 minutes or until golden brown. Remove from pan to wire rack. Drizzle Vanilla Glaze over warm rolls. Serve warm.

CINNAMON FILLING

    1/3 cup sugar
    2 teaspoons ground cinnamon

Mix ingredients.

VANILLA GLAZE

    1 cup powdered sugar
    1/2 teaspoon vanilla
    1 to 2 tablespoons milk

Mix all ingredients until smooth and thin enough to drizzle.

Serving Size: 1 Roll. Calories 285 (Calories from Fat 55); Fat 6g (Saturated 1g); Cholesterol 0mg; Sodium 300mg; Carbohydrate 56g; (Dietary Fiber 2g); Protein 4g

Raised Doughnuts

20 doughnuts

Doughnuts are popular from morning to night. For something different, try sprinkling them with powdered sugar or dipping them in melted chocolate.

    2/3 cup milk
    1/4 cup water
    1/4 cup (1/2 stick) margarine or butter, softened
    1 egg
    3 cups bread flour
    1/4 cup sugar
    1 teaspoon salt
    2 1/2 teaspoons bread machine yeast
    Vegetable oil

Measure carefully, placing all ingredients except oil in bread machine pan in the order recommended by the manufacturer.

Select Dough/Manual cycle.

Roll dough 3/8 inch thick on lightly floured board. Cut with floured doughnut cutter. Cover and let rise on board 35 to 45 minutes or until slightly raised.

Heat 2 to 3 inches oil in deep fryer or heavy 3-quart saucepan to 375°. Fry 2 or 3 doughnuts at a time 2 to 3 minutes, turning as they rise to surface, until golden brown. Remove from oil with long fork or slotted spoon. Drain on wire rack. Roll warm doughnuts in sugar, if desired.

Serving Size: 1 Doughnut Calories 235 (Calories from Fat 155); Fat 17g (Saturated 3g); Cholesterol 10mg; Sodium 140mg; Carbohydrate 19g; (Dietary Fiber 1g); Protein 3g

Garlic-Olive Spread (p. 84), Savory Roasted Pepper Bread (p. 24), Cardamom Twists (p. 75)

Terrific Toppings

Confetti Garlic Butter

About 1/2 cup

1/2 cup (1 stick) margarine or butter, softened
1 tablespoon dehydrated soup greens
1 small clove garlic, chopped

Mix all ingredients until blended. Let stand 1 hour before serving to soften soup greens.

Serving Size: 1 Tablespoon Calories 100 (Calories from Fat 100); Fat 11g (Saturated 2g); Cholesterol 0mg; Sodium 140mg; Carbohydrate 0g; (Dietary Fiber 0g); Protein 0g

Italian Parmesan Butter

About 1/2 cup

1/2 cup (1 stick) margarine or butter, softened
2 tablespoons grated Parmesan cheese
1/2 teaspoon Italian seasoning

Beat all ingredients in small bowl on high speed until blended.

Serving Size: 1 Tablespoon Calories 110 (Calories from Fat 110); Fat 12g (Saturated 3g); Cholesterol 0mg; Sodium 160mg; Carbohydrate 0g; (Dietary Fiber 0g); Protein 0g

Lemon–Poppy Seed Butter

About 1/2 cup

Lemon peel makes this spread special. The poppy seeds add a slight crunch that complements Crunchy Applesauce Bread (p. 48) and Cherry-Almond Loaf (p. 54) nicely.

1/2 cup (1 stick) margarine or butter, softened
1 tablespoon finely shredded lemon peel
1 teaspoon poppy seed

Beat all ingredients in small bowl on high speed until blended.

Serving Size: 1 Tablespoon Calories 110 (Calories from Fat 110); Fat 12g (Saturated 2g); Cholesterol 0mg; Sodium 130mg; Carbohydrate 0g; (Dietary Fiber 0g); Protein 0g

Sweet Almond Butter

About 1/2 cup

1/2 cup (1 stick) margarine or butter, softened
2 tablespoons finely chopped unblanched almonds
1 tablespoon sugar
1/4 teaspoon almond extract

Mix all ingredients until blended.

Serving Size: 1 Tablespoon Calories 115 (Calories from Fat 110); Fat 12g (Saturated 2g); Cholesterol 0mg; Sodium 130mg; Carbohydrate 2g; (Dietary Fiber 0g); Protein 0g

Cranberry-Orange Butter

About 1/2 cup

This chunky spread is a welcome addition to any breakfast setting.

1/2 cup (1 stick) margarine or butter, softened
2 tablespoons cranberry-orange relish or sauce

Mix margarine and relish until blended.

Serving Size: 1 Tablespoon Calories 105 (Calories from Fat 100); Fat 11g (Saturated 2g); Cholesterol 0mg; Sodium 140mg; Carbohydrate 2g; (Dietary Fiber 0g); Protein 0g

Sun-dried Tomato Olive Oil

About 1/2 cup

2 tablespoons drained, finely chopped sun-dried tomatoes (packed in oil)
1/3 cup extra-virgin olive oil

Stir tomatoes into oil.

Serving Size: 1 Tablespoon Calories 80 (Calories from Fat 80); Fat 9g (Saturated 1g); Cholesterol 0mg; Sodium 5mg; Carbohydrate 0g; (Dietary Fiber 0g); Protein 0g

Cheddar-Corn Spread

About 3/4 cup

1 package (3 ounces) cream cheese, softened
2 tablespoons milk
1/3 cup shredded Cheddar cheese
1/4 cup whole kernel corn
3/4 teaspoon chile powder
1 green onion, sliced

Mix cream cheese and milk until blended. Stir in remaining ingredients. Cover and refrigerate any remaining spread.

Serving Size: 1 Tablespoon Calories 45 (Calories from Fat 35); Fat 4g (Saturated 2g); Cholesterol 10mg; Sodium 55mg; Carbohydrate 1g; (Dietary Fiber 0g); Protein 1g

Nutty Olive Spread

About 1 cup

1 package (3 ounces) cream cheese, softened
2 tablespoons milk
1/2 cup finely chopped walnuts
1/4 cup finely chopped pimiento-stuffed olives

Mix cream cheese and milk until smooth. Stir in walnuts and olives. Cover and refrigerate any remaining spread.

Serving Size: 1 Tablespoon Calories 55 (Calories from Fat 40); Fat 5g (Saturated 1g); Cholesterol 5mg; Sodium 70mg; Carbohydrate 1g; (Dietary Fiber 0g); Protein 1g

Creative Condiments

Tired of the same old sandwich? Try varying the condiments and garnishes you use to add some zip to what might be an otherwise ordinary meal. Here are a few tips to help make each creation a masterpiece.

Experiment with flavored margarine or butter, mayonnaise or salad dressing, different types of mustards (Dijon, honey, sweet and sour, hot and spicy), special sauces, salsas, relishes and herbs and spices. The following suggestions will perk up any sandwich.

Barbecue Sauce
Chutney
Cream Cheese, soft
Flavored Mayonnaise
Horseradish sauce
Ketchup
Mustard, coarse-grained
Pickle relish
Ranch dressing
Salsa
Thousand Island dressing
Yogurt, plain

Cranberry-Orange Butter, Whole Wheat–Cranberry Bread (p. 39)

Basil-Pepper Spread

About 3/4 cup

Try this spread when you're looking for something to zip up your breakfast bread.

1/2 package (8-ounce size) cream cheese, softened
1 small bell pepper, finely chopped (1/2 cup)
1 tablespoon chopped fresh or 1 teaspoon dried basil leaves
2 drops red pepper sauce

Beat all ingredients in medium bowl on medium speed until fluffy. Cover and refrigerate at least 1 hour to blend flavors. Cover and refrigerate any remaining spread.

Serving Size: 1 Tablespoon Calories 35 (Calories from Fat 25); Fat 3g (Saturated 2g); Cholesterol 10mg; Sodium 30mg; Carbohydrate 1g; (Dietary Fiber 0g); Protein 1g

Garlic-Olive Spread

About 1 cup

1 1/2 cups pitted ripe olives
3 tablespoons olive oil
3 tablespoons capers, drained
1 teaspoon Italian seasoning
3 flat anchovy fillets
2 cloves garlic

Place all ingredients in food processor or blender. Cover and process, using quick on-and-off motions, until slightly coarse. Cover and refrigerate any remaining spread.

Serving Size: 1 Tablespoon Calories 40 (Calories from Fat 35); Fat 4g (Saturated 1g); Cholesterol 0mg; Sodium 140mg; Carbohydrate 1g; (Dietary Fiber 0g); Protein 0g

Curried Chutney Spread

About 1 cup

1 package (8 ounces) cream cheese, softened
1/3 cup chutney, drained and chopped
1 teaspoon curry powder
1/4 teaspoon ground mustard

Mix all ingredients until blended. Cover and refrigerate any remaining spread.

Serving Size: 1 Tablespoon Calories 55 (Calories from Fat 45); Fat 5g (Saturated 3g); Cholesterol 15mg; Sodium 45mg; Carbohydrate 2g; (Dietary Fiber 0g); Protein 1g

Great Garnishes

Make them attractive, complementary to the sandwich and edible! Fresh herbs, crisp vegetables, fruits at their finest, relishes and chutneys are good choices. Try some of these additional ideas to dress up anything on your plate.

Alfalfa Sprouts
Apple, sliced
Bacon, crisply cooked
Bell Pepper, sliced
Cabbage, leaves or shredded
Carrots, shredded
Cheese, sliced or shredded
Coleslaw
Cucumbers
Eggs, hard-cooked, sliced
Hot or sweet peppers
Lettuce
Mushrooms, sliced
Nuts, chopped
Olives, sliced
Onion, sliced
Pearl onions
Pickles, sliced
Tomato
Water chestnuts, sliced

Basil-Pepper Spread, Onion–Poppy Seed Loaf (p. 28)

Chive-Swiss Spread

About 2/3 cup

1 package (3 ounces) cream cheese, softened
2 tablespoons milk
1/2 cup finely shredded aged Swiss cheese
  (2 ounces)
1 tablespoon chopped fresh chives

Mix cream cheese and milk until smooth. Stir in cheese and chives. Cover and refrigerate any remaining spread.

Serving Size: 1 Tablespoon Calories 50 (Calories from Fat 35); Fat 4g (Saturated 3g); Cholesterol 15mg; Sodium 35mg; Carbohydrate 1g; (Dietary Fiber 0g); Protein 2g

Lemon–Cream Cheese Spread

About 1 cup

1 package (8 ounces) cream cheese, softened
1 tablespoon powdered sugar
1 teaspoon grated lemon peel
1 tablespoon lemon juice

Beat all ingredients in medium bowl on medium speed until fluffy. Cover and refrigerate any remaining spread.

Serving Size: 1 Tablespoon Calories 55 (Calories from Fat 45); Fat 5g (Saturated 3g); Cholesterol 15mg; Sodium 40mg; Carbohydrate 1g; (Dietary Fiber 0g); Protein 1g

Honey-Walnut Spread

About 1/2 cup

1 package (3 ounces) cream cheese, softened
1 tablespoon chopped walnuts
1 tablespoon honey

Mix all ingredients until blended. Cover and refrigerate any remaining spread.

Serving Size: 1 Tablespoon Calories 50 (Calories from Fat 35); Fat 4g (Saturated 2g); Cholesterol 10mg; Sodium 30mg; Carbohydrate 3g; (Dietary Fiber 0g); Protein 1g

Peanut Butter–Honey Spread

About 2/3 cup

1 package (3 ounces) cream cheese, softened
2 tablespoons milk
1/4 cup crunchy peanut butter
1 tablespoon honey

Mix cream cheese and milk until smooth. Stir in peanut butter and honey. Cover and refrigerate any remaining spread.

Serving Size: 1 Tablespoon Calories 75 (Calories from Fat 50); Fat 6g (Saturated 2g); Cholesterol 10mg; Sodium 50mg; Carbohydrate 3g; (Dietary Fiber 0g); Protein 2g

Strawberry-Rhubarb Jam

About 4 half-pints

The sharp tartness of rhubarb combines perfectly with the sweetness of plump red strawberries in this jam. You'll find the deeper the red of the rhubarb, the more beautiful the color of the jam. Be sure to use only the stalks of the rhubarb, because the leaves are poisonous.

3 cups crushed strawberries (about 1 quart whole berries)
4 cups finely chopped rhubarb (about 1 pound)
3 cups sugar
1 stick cinnamon

Mix all ingredients in Dutch oven; let stand 2 hours. Heat to boiling, stirring constantly, until mixture begins to thicken or reaches 220°, about 20 to 25 minutes. Remove from heat; quickly skim off foam. Remove cinnamon stick. Immediately pour mixture into hot sterilized jars, leaving 1/4-inch headspace. Wipe rims of jars. Seal and process in boiling water bath 5 minutes.

Serving Size: 1 Tablespoon Calories 40 (Calories from Fat 0); Fat 0g (Saturated 0g); Cholesterol 0mg; Sodium 0mg; Carbohydrate 10g; (Dietary Fiber 0g); Protein 0g

Chive-Swiss Spread, Caraway-Rye Bread (p. 42)

Strawberry Jam

About 4 half-pints

1 quart strawberries, slightly crushed
2 cups sugar
1 tablespoon lemon juice

Mix all ingredients in 3-quart saucepan; let stand 15 minutes. Heat to boiling over medium heat, stirring frequently, until sugar is dissolved. Boil about 30 minutes, stirring frequently, until mixture begins to thicken. Skim off foam quickly. Immediately pour mixture into hot sterilized jars, leaving 1/4-inch headspace. Wipe rims of jars; seal. Cool on rack 1 hour. Store in refrigerator up to 2 months.

Serving Size: 1 Tablespoon Calories 40 (Calories from Fat 0); Fat 0g (Saturated 0g); Cholesterol 0mg; Sodium 0mg; Carbohydrate 10g; (Dietary Fiber 0g); Protein 0g

Golden Raspberry Jam

About 5 half-pints

2 cups crushed golden or red raspberries (about 2 pints whole berries)
4 cups sugar
1/2 teaspoon grated lemon peel
1 tablespoon lemon juice
1 pouch (3 ounces) liquid fruit pectin

Mix raspberries and sugar. Let stand at room temperature about 10 minutes, stirring occasionally, until sugar is dissolved. Stir in lemon peel, lemon juice and pectin; continue stirring 3 to 5 minutes or until slightly thickened. Spoon into freezer containers, leaving 1/2-inch headspace. Wipe rims of containers; seal. Let stand at room temperature 24 hours. Store in refrigerator up to 3 weeks or in freezer up to 1 year. Thaw before serving.

Serving Size: 1 Tablespoon Calories 45 (Calories from Fat 0); Fat 0g (Saturated 0g); Cholesterol 0mg; Sodium mg; Carbohydrate 11g; (Dietary Fiber 0g); Protein 0g

Peach Preserves

About 6 half-pints

Capturing the fresh taste of summer peaches on a wintry morning is a wonderful reason to make these preserves! If you need to ripen the peaches for the preserves, place them in a brown paper bag and close it securely. Ripe peaches are soft and have a lovely aroma.

4 pounds peaches, peeled and sliced (about 8 cups)
6 cups sugar
1/4 cup lemon juice

Toss peaches and sugar. Cover and refrigerate at least 12 hours but no longer than 24 hours.

Heat peach mixture to boiling, stirring constantly. Rapidly boil uncovered 20 minutes. Stir in lemon juice. Boil uncovered 10 minutes longer. Immediately pour mixture into hot sterilized jars, leaving 1/4-inch headspace. Wipe rims of jars. Seal and process in boiling water bath 15 minutes.

Serving Size: 1 Tablespoon Calories 55 (Calories from Fat 0); Fat 0g (Saturated 0g); Cholesterol 0mg; Sodium 0mg; Carbohydrate 14g; (Dietary Fiber 0g); Protein 0g

Plum Preserves

About 3 half-pints

4 cups sliced plums
1 small lemon, cut lengthwise into fourths, then into paper-thin slices
2 cups sugar
1/2 cup water
1 stick cinnamon

Mix all ingredients in 3-quart saucepan. Heat to boiling over medium heat, stirring frequently, until sugar is dissolved. Boil uncovered about 35 minutes, stirring frequently, until mixture begins to thicken; remove cinnamon. Immediately pour into hot, sterilized jars, leaving 1/4-inch headspace. Wipe rims of jars; seal. Cool in rack 1 hour. Store in refrigerator up to 2 months.

Serving Size: 1 Tablespoon Calories 40 (Calories from Fat 0); Fat 0g (Saturated 0g); Cholesterol 0mg; Sodium 0mg; Carbohydrate 10g; (Dietary Fiber 0g); Protein 0g

Peach Preserves

Rosy Grape Jelly

About 5 half-pints

2 cups cranberry juice cocktail
3/4 cup grape jelly
1 package (1 3/4 ounces) powdered fruit pectin
3 1/4 cups sugar

Mix cranberry juice cocktail, grape juice and pectin in 3-quart saucepan until smooth. Heat to boiling over high heat, stirring constantly. Stir in sugar, all at once. Heat to boiling, stirring constantly. Boil and stir 1 minute; remove from heat. Quickly skim off foam. Immediately pour into hot sterilized jars. Let jars stand 1 hour. Cover with lids. Refrigerate no longer than 3 weeks, or freeze no longer than 6 months.

Serving Size: 1 Tablespoon Calories 35 (Calories from Fat 0); Fat 0g (Saturated 0g); Cholesterol 0mg; Sodium 0mg; Carbohydrate 9g; (Dietary Fiber 0g); Protein 0g

Herbed Tangerine Jelly

About 4 half-pints

2 tablespoons dried marjoram leaves or whole cloves
2 cups boiling water
1/2 can (12-ounce size) frozen tangerine juice concentrate, thawed
1 package (1 3/4 ounces) powdered fruit pectin
3 3/4 cups sugar

Wrap marjoram tightly in cheesecloth. Place in 4-cup measure with 2 cups boiling water. Cover and let stand 10 minutes. To extract flavor, squeeze liquid from cheesecloth into water and discard cheesecloth. Add enough water to herb water to measure 2 cups.

Mix herb water, tangerine juice concentrate and pectin in 3-quart saucepan until pectin is dissolved. Heat to boiling, stirring constantly. Stir in sugar. Heat to rolling boil, stirring constantly; remove from heat. Immediately pour into hot, sterilized jars or glasses or freezer containers, leaving 1/2-inch headspace. Wipe rims of jars. Cover tightly; cool. Store in refrigerator up to 1 month or in freezer up to 2 months.

Apple-Pepper Jelly: Omit marjoram and first step. Substitute 1 can (6 ounces) frozen apple juice for the tangerine juice concentrate; the 2 cups water do not need to be boiling. Stir in 1 to 2 tablespoons crushed red pepper with the sugar. Strain before filling jars, if desired.

Serving Size: 1 Tablespoon Calories 50 (Calories from Fat 0); Fat 0g (Saturated 0g); Cholesterol 0mg; Sodium 0mg; Carbohydrate 13g; (Dietary Fiber 0g); Protein 0g

Cranberry Conserve

About 5 half-pints

2 cup packed brown sugar
2 cup water
2 packages (12 ounces each) cranberries
2 tablespoons grated orange peel
4 oranges, peeled and chopped
2 apples, peeled and chopped
1 cup chopped nuts

Mix brown sugar and water in Dutch oven., Heat to boiling; boil 1 minute. Stir in remaining ingredients except nuts. Heat to boiling; boil rapidly about 20 minutes or until cranberries pop and mixture thickens.Stir in nuts. Immediately pour into hot, sterilized jars, leaving 1/2-inch headspace. Wipe rims of jars. Cover tightly; cool. Store in refrigerator or freezer up to 3 months. Thaw before serving.

Serving Size: 1 Tablespoon Calories 40 (Calories from Fat 10); Fat 1g (Saturated 0g); Cholesterol 0mg; Sodium 2mg; Carbohydrate 8g; (Dietary Fiber 0g); Protein 0g

Apple Butter

About 3 half-pints

This is a tasty addition for any slice of bread. And because it is low-fat, it is a great replacement for butter.

    4 quarts apple cider or juice
    12 cups pared, cored and quartered cooking
        apples (about 4 pounds)
    2 cups sugar
    1 teaspoon ground ginger
    1 teaspoon ground cinnamon
    1/2 teaspoon ground cloves

Heat apple cider to boiling in 5-quart Dutch oven. Boil uncovered until cider measures 2 quarts, about 1 1/4 hours. Add apples. Heat to boiling; reduce heat. Simmer uncovered, stirring frequently, until apples are very soft, about 1 hour.

Press through sieve or food mill, or mash with potato masher just until smooth. Stir in remaining ingredients. Heat to boiling; reduce heat. Simmer uncovered, stirring frequently, until no liquid separates from pulp, about 2 hours. Heat to boiling.

Immediately pour mixture into hot sterilized jars, leaving 1/4-inch headspace. Wipe rims of jars. Seal and process in boiling water bath 10 minutes.

Serving Size: 1 Tablespoon Calories 90 (Calories from Fat 0); Fat 0g (Saturated 0g); Cholesterol 0mg; Sodium 5mg; Carbohydrate 22g; (Dietary Fiber 0g); Protein 0g

Lemon Curd

About 2 cups

    1 cup sugar
    2 teaspoons finely shredded lemon peel
    1 cup lemon juice (about 5 large lemons)
    3 tablespoons firm margarine or butter, cut up
    3 eggs, slightly beaten

Mix sugar, lemon peel and lemon juice in heavy 1 1/2-quart saucepan. Stir in margarine and eggs. Cook over medium heat about 8 minutes, stirring constantly, until mixture thickens and coats back of spoon (do not boil). Immediately pour into 1-pint container or two 1-cup containers. Cover and refrigerate no longer than 2 months.

Serving Size: 1 Tablespoon Calories 50 (Calories from Fat 20); Fat 2g (Saturated 0g); Cholesterol 20mg; Sodium 20mg; Carbohydrate 7g; (Dietary Fiber 0g); Protein 1g

Metric Conversion Guide

Volume

U.S. Units	Canadian Metric	Australian Metric
1/4 teaspoon	1 mL	1 ml
1/2 teaspoon	2 mL	2 ml
1 teaspoon	5 mL	5 ml
1 tablespoon	15 mL	20 ml
1/4 cup	50 mL	60 ml
1/3 cup	75 mL	80 ml
1/2 cup	125 mL	125 ml
2/3 cup	150 mL	170 ml
3/4 cup	175 mL	190 ml
1 cup	250 mL	250 ml
1 quart	1 liter	1 liter
1 1/2 quarts	1.5 liters	1.5 liters
2 quarts	2 liters	2 liters
2 1/2 quarts	2.5 liters	2.5 liters
3 quarts	3 liters	3 liters
4 quarts	4 liters	4 liters

Weight

U.S. Units	Canadian Metric	Australian Metric
1 ounce	30 grams	30 grams
2 ounces	55 grams	60 grams
3 ounces	85 grams	90 grams
4 ounces (1/4 pound)	115 grams	125 grams
8 ounces (1/2 pound)	225 grams	225 grams
16 ounces (1 pound)	455 grams	500 grams
1 pound	455 grams	1/2 kilogram

Note: The recipes in this cookbook have not been developed or tested using metric measures. When converting recipes to metric, some variations in quality may be noted.

Measurements

Inches	Centimeters
1	2.5
2	5.0
3	7.5
4	10.0
5	12.5
6	15.0
7	17.5
8	20.5
9	23.0
10	25.5
11	28.0
12	30.5
13	33.0
14	35.5
15	38.0

Temperatures

Fahrenheit	Celsius
32°	0°
212°	100°
250°	120°
275°	140°
300°	150°
325°	160°
350°	180°
375°	190°
400°	200°
425°	220°
450°	230°
475°	240°
500°	260°

Index

Numbers in *italics* refer to photos.

A

Almond
  -Apricot Bread, 49, *73*
  Butter, Sweet, 81
  -Cherry Loaf, 54
  –Chocolate Chip Bread, 54, *55*
  Honey–Whole Wheat Bread, 37
  -Orange Rolls, *19*
Amaretto-Coffee Bread, 56
Apple
  Bread, Spicy, *36*, 48
  Butter, 91
  -Pepper Jelly, 90
Applesauce Bread, Crunchy, 48
Apricot-Almond Bread, 49, *73*
Apricot Glaze, 49

B

Banana–Chocolate Chip Bread,
  36, 50
Basil-Pepper Spread, 84, *85*
Blueberry-Lemon Loaf, 51
Bread
  baking tips, 68
  cutting tips, 30
  5 steps to, 5–6
  guide to, 8–9
  storing, 60
Bread Crumbs, 49
Bread Pudding, 50
Bread toppings, 18, 50
Breadsticks, Savory, 71
Breadsticks, Wild Rice, 72, *73*
Brioche, Miniature, 70
Buttermilk Bread, 14
Butters
  Apple, 91
  Confetti Garlic, 81
  Cranberry-Orange, 82
  Italian Parmesan, 81

Lemon–Poppy Seed, 81
Sweet Almond, 81

C

Cajun Bread, 25
Calzones, 70
Caramelized Onion Focaccia,
  62, *63*
Caramel-Pecan Rolls, 75
Caraway-Rye Bread, 42, *87*
Cardamom Twists, 75, *80*
Challah Braid, 62
Cheddar
  -Corn Spread, *44*, 82
  -Olive Bread, 27, *73*
  -Onion Bread, 28
  -Taco Bread, 29
Cheese Loaf, Savory, 22
Cheese Pizza, Favorite, 64, *65*
Cheesy Garlic Monkey Bread, 64
Cherry-Almond Loaf, 54
Chive-Swiss Spread, 86, *87*
Chocolate Chip–Almond Bread,
  54, *55*
Chocolate Chip–Banana Bread,
  36, 50
Christmas coffee cake, 57
Chutney Spread, Curried, 84
Cinnamon
  Filling, 75, 79
  -Raisin Bread, 15
  Rolls, Glazed, *78*, 79
Classic White Loaf, 13
Coconut-Pecan Braid, 74
Coffee-Amaretto Bread, 56
Coffee Cake, Fruited, *76*, 77
Coffee cake, Julekage, 57
Condiments, 82
Confetti Garlic Butter, 81
Corn Bread, Jalapeño, *44*, 45

Cottage Dill Bread, 22, *23*
Crabmeat Pizza, 66
Cranberry
  Conserve, 90
  -Orange Butter, 82, *83*
  –Whole Wheat Bread, 39, *83*
Cream Cheese–Lemon Spread, 86
Croutons, homemade, 41, 50
Crumb toppings, 18, 50
Crunchy Applesauce Bread, 48
Currant-Oatmeal Bread, 43
Curried Chutney Spread, 84
Cutting bread machine loaves, 10

D

Deep-Dish Pizza with Fresh
  Tomato Sauce, 67
Dijon-Thyme Bread, 17
Dilled Brown Rice Bread, 26
Double Apricot–Almond Bread,
  49, *73*
Double Mustard–Beer Bread, 17
Doughnuts, 79

E

Easy Family Pizza, 67

F

Family Pizza with Fresh Tomato
  Sauce, 67
Favorite Cheese Pizza, 64, *65*
Fireside Cheddar-Olive Bread,
  27, *73*
Flours, 6–7
Focaccia, Caramelized Onion,
  62, *63*

Focaccia, Rosemary, 66
French
  Baguettes, *58*, 59
  Onion Tart, 60, *61*
  Toast, 50
  Twists, 72
Fresh Herb Bread, 33
Fresh Tomato Sauce, 67
Fruited Coffee Cake, *76*, 77

G

Garlic
  -Basil Bread, 27
  Bread, Roasted, 32
  Bread Topping, 18
  Butter, 81
  -Olive Spread, *80*, 84
Garnishes, 84
Gingered Pear Bread, 51
Glazed Cinnamon Rolls, *78*, 79
Golden Raspberry Jam, 88
Great Granola Bread, 35
Greek Olive Bread, 29

H

Harvest Loaf, 18, *19*
Herb Bread, Fresh, 33
Herbed Tangerine Jelly, 90
Homemade Croutons, 41
Honey-Sunflower Loaf, *12*, 35
Honey-Walnut Spread, 86

I

Italian Parmesan Butter, 81
Italian Salami Sandwich Loaf,
  68, *69*

J

Jalapeño Corn Bread, *44*, 45
Jams and preserves
  Apple-Pepper Jelly, 90
  Cranberry Conserve, 90
  Golden Raspberry, 88

Herbed Tangerine, 90
Peach, 88, *89*
Plum, 88
Rosy Grape Jelly, 90
Strawberry, 88
Strawberry-Rhubarb, 86
Julekage, 57

L

Leftovers, storing, 60
Lemon
  -Anise Loaf, 53
  -Blueberry Loaf, 51
  –Cream Cheese Spread, 86
  Curd, 91
  –Poppy Seed Butter, 81

M

Menus, 11
Metric conversion guide, 92
Miniature Brioche, 70
Multigrain Loaf, *46*, 47

N

Nutty Olive Spread, 82

O

Oatmeal Bread, with Currants, 43
Oatmeal-Pecan Loaf, *38*, 43
Olive
  Bread, Greek-style, 29
  -Cheddar Bread, 73
  -Garlic Spread, 84
  Spread, Nutty, 82
Onion
  -Cheddar Bread, 28
  Focaccia, Caramelized, 62, *63*
  –Poppy Seed Loaf, 28, *85*
  Tart, French-style, 60, *61*
  Topping, 60
Orange
  -Almond Rolls, 19
  -Cranberry Butter, 82, *83*

Rolls, Sticky, 77
–Whole Wheat Bread, *38*, 39
Oven Stuffing, 50

P

Panettone, 53
Parmesan
  Butter, Italian-style, 81
  -Garlic Twists, 74
  –Pine Nut Bread, 24
Peach Preserves, 88, *89*
Peanut Butter Bread, 16
Peanut Butter–Honey Spread,
  36, 86
Pear Bread, Gingered, 51
Pecan
  -Caramel Rolls, 75
  -Coconut Braid, 74
  -Oatmeal Loaf, *38*, 43
Pepperoni Pizza Bread, 20, *21*
Pesto-Tomato Bread, 30, *31*
Pineapple Aloha Bread, 52
Pizza
  Bread, Pepperoni, 20, *21*
  Favorite Cheese, 64, *65*
  with Fresh Tomato Sauce, 67
  Shrimp and Scallop, 66
Plum Preserves, 88
Potato-Chive Bread, 20
Praline Sweet Potato Bread, 34
Preserves. *See* Jams and preserves
Pumpkin–Whole Wheat Bread,
  40, 41

R

Raised Doughnuts, 79
Ranch Bread, 15
Raspberry Jam, 88
Rhubarb-Strawberry Jam, 86
Roasted Garlic Bread, 32
Roasted Pepper Bread, Savory,
  24, *80*
Rolls
  Caramel-Pecan, 75
  Cardamom Twists, 75, *80*
  French Twists, 72
  Glazed Cinnamon, *78*, 79

Orange-Almond, 19
Parmesan-Garlic Twists, 74
Sticky Orange, 77
Whole Wheat Dinner, 71
Rosemary Focaccia, 66
Rosy Grape Jelly, 90
Rye Bread, Caraway, 42, *87*
Rye Loaf, Sauerkraut, 42

S

Salami Sandwich Loaf, Italian-style,
    68, *69*
Sally Lunn, 14
Salsa Bread, *23*, 25
Sandwich ideas, 16
Sauerkraut-Rye Loaf, 42
Savory
    Breadsticks, 71
    Calzones, 70
    Cheese Loaf, 22
    Roasted Pepper Bread, 24, *80*
Shrimp and Scallop Pizza, 66

Spicy Apple Bread, *36*, 48
Spreads
    Basil-Pepper, 84, *85*
    Cheddar-Corn, 82
    Chive-Swiss, 86, *87*
    Curried Chutney, 84
    Garlic-Olive, 84
    Honey-Walnut, 86
    Lemon–Cream Cheese, 86
    Lemon Curd, 91
    Nutty Olive, 82
    Peanut Butter–Honey, *36*, 86
Sticky Orange Rolls, 77
Storing bread machine loaves, 10
Strawberry Jam, 88
Strawberry-Rhubarb Jam, 86
Stuffing, 50
Sun-dried Tomato Olive Oil,
    58, 82
Sunflower Loaf, Honey, *12*, 35
Sweet
    Almond Butter, 81
    Lemon-Anise Loaf, 53
    Potato Bread, Praline, 34
Swiss Cheese–Chive Spread, 86, *87*

T

Taco-Cheddar Bread, 29
Tangerine Jelly, Herbed, 90
Tomato-Pesto Bread, 30, *31*
Tomato Sauce, Fresh, 67
Toppings from breads, 18, 50
Trail Mix Bread, 26

V

Vanilla Glaze, 79

W

Walnut-Honey Spread, 86
White Bread, Classic, 13
Whole Wheat Bread
    Almond Honey, 37
    Cranberry, 39, *83*
    Orange, *38*, 39
    Pumpkin, *40*, 41
Whole Wheat Dinner Rolls, 71
Wild Rice Breadsticks, 72, *73*